Norfolk at Christmas

Compiled by
Moya Leighton

LUCAS BOOKS

Norfolk at Christmas

© Copyright 2003

First Published by
LUCAS BOOKS 2003

ISBN 1903797-07-1

British Library Cataloguing in Publication Data
A catalogue record for this book is available from the British Library

Printed in the UK
by Brackenbury Associates - Ipswich

For Hazel, Emma and Brenda
with thanks.

Contents

Introduction

Eclogue Sylvia Townsend Warner

The Spirit of Christmas Past

The Nativity Margery Kempe of Lynn

From *Revelations of Divine Love* Lady Julian of Norwich

Letters of the Paston Family Edited by Roger Virgoe

Parson Woodforde's frolic for Christmas Eric Fowler

The Norfolk Hero: Vice-Admiral Horatio, Lord Nelson
Carola Oman

The Rev. Benjamin Armstrong of Dereham

The man who wrote *King Solomon's Mines*

A Farmers Year: 1898 H Rider Haggard

Christmas 1909: Flashman at Sandringham
George MacDonald Fraser

A Vision of Christmas: Christmas 1914 Henry Williamson

A Sprig of Holly: Christmas 1918 Adrian Bell

The Sad Tale of Humpty Dumpty Robert Bagshaw

Old Year's Night at Fenchurch St. Paul Dorothy Sayers

The Worst Trip that Henry Blogg ever made Cyril Jolly

Peter Scott and *Kazarka* Peter Scott

The Williamson Family Christmas at Stiffkey
Henry Williamson

A Wartime Christmas beside the River Waveney
Lilias Rider Haggard

Christmas Eve at St. Michael's Church, Barton Turf
William Rivière

Winter at Great Eye Folly, Salthouse
Sylvia Townsend Warner

A Countryman's Christmas Notebooks 1953-1977
Adrian Bell

"It was a house that lent itself to Christmas": Edward Seago and the Dutch House, Ludham — Jean Goodman

Tiki - The Wanderer — David Chaffe

All Part of the Service: Behind the Scenes in a National Trust Restaurant — Mary Mackie

Christmas Time on Bishop Peter's Pilgrimage — The Right Reverend Peter Nott

Christmas — John Betjeman

Town Mourns as Tragic Events Unfold: Deep Sadness and Despair at Wells

The Spirit of Christmas Present — John Nursey

The Spirit of Christmas Present

"I Carn't Wairt ter See Har Fearce..." — Michael Brindid

Happiness Doesn't Have a Price Tag — Marianne Gibbs

Don't You *Dare* Buy Me a Pixie Hood — Sharon Griffiths

The Spirit of Christmas to Come

The Best Present Ever — Reverend Janice Scott

For Unto Us a Child is Born...

Inspiring Words of Advent Anthems — Reverend Jack Burton

The Man Born to be King

On the Eve of Saint Thomas — Sylvia Townsend Warner

Christmas Eve at Mangreen — Maureen Harris

That Speshul Bearby — Reverend Colin Riches

My Christmas Wishes for you — Maureen Harris

Epiphany

The Guiding Star is Common Humanity — Reverend Jack Burton

Deck the Halls with Boughs of Holly

Hire a Spruce - and Let it Live

Norfolk Tarkies — Henry Williamson

Turkey Country — Michael Pollitt

Turkey Farmer is Latest Food Hero — Michael Pollitt

Feathers Fly - Far and Wide...

Festive Recipes

Festive Recipe is Always Delicious   Charles Roberts
Christmas Cards and Christmas Stamps
Season's Greetings from Robin Redbreast   Moss Taylor
Christmas Crackers
Father Christmas
…And They Just Lapped Up the Fun   Rachel Buller
On Having Guests to Stay   Adrian Bell
Service Launch to MFV *Toriki*   Allen Frary
At Christmas   John Nursey
Making Paper Chains   Adrian Bell
A Norfolk Boy Born on Christmas Day   Michael Home
Christmas Day Service at Happisburgh - RNLI Style
Joy and Charles Boldero's Boxing Day Walk at Brancaster
Boxing Day Rescue at Hunstanton
The Sales   Adrian Bell
Old Year's Night
Start the New Year with Plenty of Cheer   Sharon Griffiths
The Wicked Squire of Ranworth   Charles Sampson
Ringing in the New Year at St. Michael's Church, Beccles
                                                 Adrian Bell
First Day of the Year Seldom Disappoints   Moss Taylor
Pantomime Time at the Theatre Royal   Adrian Bell
Twelfth Night
Holly   Grace Corne

Introduction

However impartial one tries to be, a collection of this nature must, to some extent, be subjective. I have included extracts from many of Adrian Bell's *Countryman's Notebooks*, partly because I am secretary of The Adrian Bell Society, and our 250 members can't be the only readers still to enjoy his writing, and partly because he recorded the tiny details of everyday life in lively and articulate words every Saturday for thirty years.

I started by searching my own bookshelves and then moved to those of the public libraries and the *Eastern Daily Press*. I searched reference books to discover writers hitherto known only by name. I was enchanted by the letters, diaries and poems of Sylvia Townsend Warner. I read Henry Rider Haggard for the first time. David Chaffe's *Stormforce* caught my eye in a Cromer book shop and I found Peter Scott's *The Eye of the Wind*, which I had last read in the 1960s, in a charity shop.

I would like to thank everyone who has helped me in my search for words and pictures to show Norfolk at Christmas.

I have also enjoyed many of the pleasures of Christmas in Norfolk over the years:

I attended the Christmas Morning Service in Norwich Cathedral and marvelled at the purity of the singing and the Midnight Service in a village where a painted angel with bagpipes looked down on the celebrants at communion and everyone sang.
I carried the collecting box as we sang carols for charity - they wouldn't let me sing.

I fired at a moving line of battered tin ducks at the fair on the old Cattlemarket on Boxing Day, with a fair degree of success, as the first snowflakes fell.

I have seen many pantomimes at the Theatre Royal and felt the disappointment as children grew out of their pantomime years. I painted a backcloth for Cinderella's kitchen and spoke my three lines on an amateur stage.

I spent a day with Santa at Weybourne Station and shared his welcoming fire.

I was enchanted by wagtails going to their roost in the tree near Debenhams' windows.

I made robes for an angel and shed a tear or two at a primary school's Nativity play, and felt a lump in my throat as young voices hit most of the right notes.

I sledged in the snow at an unsuitably mature age. I walked, with the Ramblers' and alone, and rowed the lonely length of Sutton Broad in the sunlight of a frosty New Year's Day.

I have enjoyed the delights of Norfolk at Christmas.

I hope this book rekindles happy memories for each and every one of you.

Moya Leighton

Eclogue

'Neighbour, let us to our church go
This Christmas Eve,
To see the shepherds and the kings kneel low
And Jesus in Mary's sleeve
And Joseph standing by well-pleased.'

'Babe nor mother should we find
This winter's night.
Our church now belongs to a king whose mind
Is grown too wise to delight
In toys and images like these.'

'Neighbour, let us to the tavern go
This Christmas Eve,
And kiss Nan under the mistletoe,
And give the mummers good leave
To quench their roaring thirst in our bowl.'

'Mirth nor mummers should we find
This winter's night;
For Oliver's men are strict to bind
In stocked or pilloried plight
Players of wanton games like these.'

'Neighbour, let us to our neighbours go
This Christmas Eve,
And raise those tunes of long-ago,
And a drink or a shilling receive
In thanks for the good news we have told.'

'Drink nor shilling should we find
This winter's night;

Norfolk at Christmas

For schoolmistress teaches how unrefined
Must sound to all ears polite
Such old-time country staves as these.'

'Neighbour, let us to the pictures go
This Christmas Eve,
And see a lady her garters show,
And a cunning thief deceive,
And the townsfolk sitting there well-pleased.'

Sylvia Townsend Warner - *Collected Poems*

The Adoration of the Infant Christ by the Magi. by Martin Schwarz 1480.
Situated in the Jesus Chapel it formed part of a triptych of which the
wings are lost.   *Norwich Cathedral*

The Spirit of Christmas Past

Sylvia Townsend Warner's poem charts the stormy shift of opinion on the appropriate way to behave at Christmas. King Henry VIII wrested power and property from the monasteries, thereby hastening the secularisation of Christmas, Oliver Cromwell's austere followers destroyed graven images and defaced church screens, and Parson Woodforde's contemporaries relished the flavour of Norfolk's black-feathered turkeys. The Victorians, who knew all there is to know about spectacular consumption and 'retail therapy', reinvented Christmas in their own image and the Twentieth Century added cinema, television, computer games and oven-ready turkey.

Our first glimpse of the Christmas story is through the eyes of Margery Kempe (c.1373-c.1440) of Lynn. This mother of fourteen undertook numerous pilgrimages, to Jerusalem, Rome and the holy places of the known world, and dictated the story of her religious experiences and travels. If she had recorded her everyday travels with the same meticulous detail as her spiritual experiences, we would have been left with the *Rough Guide to the Pilgrim Trail*. As it is, we can only imagine the hardship and dangers she experienced.

Margery Kempe's account of the Nativity shows the down-to-earth practicality of one for whom childbirth, however holy this birth may be, held no mysteries. In this extract she refers to herself as "the creature":

The Nativity: Margery Kempe of Lynn

Another day, this creature gave herself up to meditation as she had been commanded before, and she lay still, not knowing what she might best think of. Then she said to our Lord Jesus Christ, 'Jesus, what shall I think about?'

Our Lord Jesus answered in her mind, 'Daughter, think of my mother, for she is the cause of all the grace that you have.'

And then at once she saw St Anne, great with child, and then she prayed St Anne to let her be her maid and her servant. And presently our Lady was born, and then she busied herself to take the child to herself and look after her until she was twelve years of age, with good food and drink, with fair white clothing and white kerchiefs. And then she said to the blessed child, 'My lady, you shall be the mother of God.'

The blessed child answered and said, 'I wish I were worthy to be the handmaiden of her that should conceive the son of God.'

The creature said, 'I pray you, my lady, if that grace befall you, do not discontinue with my service.'

The blessed child went away for a certain time - the creature remaining still in contemplation - and afterwards came back again and said, 'Daughter, now I have become the mother of God.'

And then the creature fell down on her knees with great reverence and great weeping and said, 'I am not worthy, my lady, to do you service.'

'Yes, daughter,' she said, 'follow me - I am well pleased with your service.'

Then she went forth with our Lady and with Joseph, bearing with her a flask of wine sweetened with honey and spices. Then they went forth to Elizabeth, St John the Baptist's mother, and when they met together Mary and Elizabeth reverenced each other, and so they dwelled together with great grace and gladness for twelve weeks. And then St John was born, and our Lady took him up from the ground with all reverence and gave him to his mother, saying of him that he would be a holy man, and blessed him.

Afterwards they took leave of each other with compassionate tears. And then the creature fell down on her knees to St Elizabeth, and begged her that she would pray for her to our Lady so that she might still serve and please her.

'Daughter,' said Elizabeth, 'it seems to me that you do your duty very well.'

And then the creature went forth with our Lady to Bethlehem and procured lodgings for her every night with great reverence, and our Lady was received with good cheer. She also begged for our Lady pieces of fair white cloth and kerchiefs to swaddle her son in when he was born; and when Jesus was born she arranged bedding for our Lady to lie on with her blessed son. And later she begged food for our Lady and her blessed child. Afterwards she swaddled him, weeping bitter tears of compassion, mindful of the painful death that he would suffer for the love of sinful men, saying to him, 'Lord, I shall treat you gently; I will not bind you tightly. I pray you not to be displeased with me.'

And afterwards on the twelfth day, when three kings came with their gifts and worshipped our Lord Jesus Christ in his mother's lap, this creature, our Lady's handmaiden, beholding the whole process in contemplation, wept marvellously sorely. And when she saw that they wished to take their leave to go home again to their country, she could not bear that they should go from the presence of our Lord, and in her wonder that they wished to leave she cried so grievously that it was amazing.

And soon after, an angel came and commanded our Lady and Joseph to go from the country of Bethlehem into Egypt. Then this creature went forth with our Lady, finding her lodging day by day with great reverence, with many sweet thoughts and high meditations...

The Nativity. 15th century roof boss from the North Transept, Norwich Cathedral.

Photograph by Julia Hedgecoe.

The Friends of Norwich Cathedral

Margery Kempe lived at the same time as Lady Julian of Norwich, and the two devout women met on one occasion:

And then she was commanded by our Lord to go to an anchoress in the same city who was called Dame Julian. And so she did, and told her about the grace, that God had put into her soul, of compunction, contrition, sweetness and devotion, compassion with holy meditation and high contemplation, and very many holy speeches and converse that our Lord spoke to her soul, and also many wonderful revelations, which she described to the anchoress to find out if there were any deception in them, for the anchoress was expert in such things and could give good advice.

Margery Kempe - *The Book of Margery Kempe.*
(Translated by B.A. Windeatt 1994)

Nothing is known of this meeting but a dramatist could surely conjure something fascinating from the encounter of these two women of widely different backgrounds and experience:

Lady Julian (c. 1342-1413) wrote *Sixteen Revelations of Divine Love.* She was a mystic and has been described as an anchoress, but she lived in the heart of Norwich and did not cut herself off from other people. She offered counsel and assurance of the love of God, so that "all shall be well". Her eleventh and twelfth revelations concern her visions of the Virgin Mary:

Lady Julian of Norwich

...Jesus said: *Wilt thou see her?* methought it was the most pleasing word that He might have given me of her, with that ghostly Shewing that He gave me of her. For our Lord shewed me nothing in special but our Lady Saint Mary; and her He shewed three times. The first was as she was with Child; the second was as she was in her sorrows under the Cross; the third is as she is now in pleasing, worship, and joy.

And after this our Lord shewed Himself more glorified, as to my sight, than I saw Him before...wherein I was learned that our soul shall never have rest till it cometh to Him, knowing that He is fulness of joy, homely and courteous, blissful and very life.

Lady Julian of Norwich - *Revelations of Divine Love.* 1373

The Paston Family

A unique collection of documents relating to one prominent Norfolk family survived through the ages and was eventually published. These Paston letters chronicle a time of uncertainty, feuding and fighting, when might was often considered right, and the legal profession grew rich from the ensuing litigation.

It was an age of large families, high infant and maternal mortality, limited medical and gynaecological knowledge and a small repertoire of Paston Christian names. Christmas was a great religious feast, a celebration of the passing of the shortest day of the year and a time to eat well and wear new finery if one could.

When it looked as if young John Paston and Margaret Mauteby were to be married, the bride-to-be's wardrobe was augmented:

Agnes Paston to William Paston   April 1436/40
Paston

The Flight into Egypt. 15th century roof boss from the North Transept, Norwich Cathdral.

Photograph by Julia Hedgecoe.

The Friends of Norwich Cathedral

…The gown needs to be had, and of colour it should be a goodly blue or else a bright sanguine [blood-red]…

By Christmas of 1441 John and Margaret were married and Margaret was considering her expanding waistline, her difficulty in sleeping comfortably and the forthcoming birth of her first child. Little in her wardrobe now fits. As was the convention of the day, she refers to William and Agnes Paston, her in-laws, as her father and mother. Her eldest son, John, was born early in 1442.

Margaret Paston to John Paston   14 December 1441
Oxnead

Right reverent and worshipful husband, I recommend me to you, desiring heartily to hear of your welfare…praying you to understand that my mother sent to my father at London for a gown cloth of musterdevillers [a grey woollen cloth] to make a gown for me…I pray you, if it be not bought, that you will vouchsafe to buy it and send it home as soon as you may, for I have no gown to wear this winter but my black and my green…and that is so cumbrous that I am weary of it. As for the girdle that my father promised me, I spoke to him of it a little before he went to London last, and he said to me that the fault was in you, that you would not think thereupon to have it made; but I suppose that is not so: he said it but for an excuse. I pray you, if you will take it upon you, that you will vouchsafe to have it made before you come home for I had never more need of it than now; for I have grown so slim that I cannot be girt into any girdle I have except one.

Elizabeth Peverel has been sick 15 or 16 weeks with the sciatica but she has sent my mother word by Kate that she would come here when my time comes from God, though she should have to be wheeled in a barrow. John Damme was here and my mother discovered me [my pregnancy] to him and he said, by his troth, that he was not more glad of anything he had heard for a twelvemonth than of this. I may no longer live by my craft [deception], for I am discovered of all men that see me...I pray that you will wear the ring with the image of St. Margaret that I sent you for a remembrance till you come home; you have left me such a remembrance that makes me to think upon you both day and night when I would sleep.

In September 1443 John was in London, at the Inner Temple, recovering from serious illness, and Margaret was pregnant again. What kind of Christmas did they have? Did Margaret ever get a scarlet gown?

Margaret Paston to John Paston   28 September 1443
Oxnead

Right worshipful husband, I recommend me to you, heartily desiring to hear of your welfare, thanking God for your mending of the great dis-ease that you have had. And I thank you for the letter that you sent me, for, by my troth, my mother and I were not at ease from the time that we knew of your sickness till we knew verily of your mending. My mother promised another image of wax of the weight of yourself to Our Lady of Walsingham and she sent 4 nobles to the 4 orders of friars at Norwich to pray for you; and I have promised pilgrimages to be made for you to Walsingham and to St. Leonard's [Priory, Norwich]. By my troth, I never had so heavy a season from the time that I knew of your sickness until I knew of your amending, and still my heart is not at great ease, nor shall be until I know that you are truly well.

My father Garneys sent me word that he should be here the next week and my uncle also, and play here with their hawks; and they would have me home with them but, so God help me, I shall excuse myself from going thither if I may, for I suppose that I shall have tidings more readily from you here than I should there.
I shall send my mother a token that she gave me, for I suppose the

time is come that I should send for her if I keep the promise that I have made...

I pray you heartily that you will vouchsafe to send me a letter as hastily as you may, if writing be no disease to you, and that you will vouchsafe to send me word how your sore does. I would rather you were at home now, if it were to your ease and if your sore might be as well looked to here as it is where you are, than have a gown, though it were of scarlet. I pray you, if your sore be whole and that you may endure to ride, that when my father comes to London you ask leave to come home when the horse shall be sent home again, for I hope that you would be kept as tenderly here as you are in London. Almighty God have you in his keeping and send you health...

Norwich Cathedral
    from the Upper Green.

Photograph by
    Deirdre Grierson
Friends of Norwich Cathedral

Over the years the family grew in size and importance. The death of Sir John Falstof of Caister, a relation of Margaret's, brought property and security but presented problems of etiquette. Margaret asked advice on the degree of sobriety appropriate to the Christmas festivities from Lady Morley.

Margaret Paston to John Paston   24 December 1459

Please you to know that I sent your eldest son to my Lady Morley to have knowledge what sports were used in her house at Christmas next following after the decease of my lord, her husband. And she said that there were no disguisings [acting], nor harping, luting or singing, nor any lewd sports, but just playing at the tables [backgammon] and chess and cards. Such sports she gave her folk leave to play and no other... I sent your younger son to Lady Stapleton's and she said the same as Lady Morley, that this had been the practice in places of worship [honourable households] where she had been...

Abridged from *Private Life in the Fifteenth Century: Illustrated Letters of The Paston Family* - Edited by Roger Virgoe. 1989

The centuries passed. The Tudors feasted, listened to madrigals, watched masques, wore jewel-encrusted clothes, carried pomanders to protect themselves from stench and plague, plotted on the chessboard of international intrigue and extended the limits of the known world. The Stuarts came to the throne, uniting England and Scotland, and England suffered civil war, regicide, religious intolerance and the hunting and slaughter of men of religion and old women who were thought to be witches. The estates of Blickling, Felbrigg and Houghton changed the face of the Norfolk landscape and, with Hanoverian kings now on the throne, a bachelor clergyman living in a quiet Norfolk parish wrote a diary.
The Reverend James Woodforde (1740-1803), Parson Woodforde of Weston Longville, is the ideal companion for the Christmas season.

He was born in Ansford in Somerset and in 1774 was presented to the living of Weston Longville by New College, Oxford. He moved to his new parish in May 1776. Although not born in Norfolk, he has become a man of Norfolk by adoption and his diary transports us to another age and way of life.

In this extract from the *Eastern Daily Press*, Eric Fowler, writing as Jonathan Mardle, pays tribute to the diary-writing incumbent of Weston Longville rectory:

In December 1963, Eric Fowler took a seasonal excursion down one of his favourite Norfolk byways.

Parson Woodforde's Frolic for Christmas

Diaries are delightful reading, but they are books to be dipped into rather than read from cover to cover. A seasonal pleasure is to flick over the pages of Parson Woodforde's Diary until you come to December, and see how that convivial soul spent his Christmases between 1774 and 1803, when he was rector of Weston Longville.

Woodforde's festivities began in the first week in December, when the farmers and smallholders of the parish, to the number of 20 or 30, came to the rectory to pay their tithes for the year - and did so with the better grace because the parson celebrated the occasion by giving them a dinner, which he called his frolic. The feast started at two o'clock in the afternoon, and it was Woodforde's endeavour, in which he was not always successful, to get all his guests more or less soberly out of the house by 10. He dined with the most substantial farmers in what he called his great parlour. Smallholders and cottagers were entertained, along with the parish clerk, in the kitchen. Nancy, the bachelor parson's niece, housekeeper, companion, tease and occasionally torment, dined in solitude in the study, Woodforde tells us in 1784:

"I gave them for Dinner some Salt Fish, a Leg of Mutton boiled and Capers, a fine Loin of Beef roasted, and plenty of plumb and plain Puddings. They that dined in the Kitchen had no Punch or Wine, but strong Beer and Table Beer, and would not come into Parlour to have Punch etc. They drank in Parlour 7 Bottles of Port Wine, and both my large Bowls of Rum Punch, each of which took 2 bottles of Rum to make. Forster went away the most disguised of any. In the Kitchen they were all cheerfully merry but none much disguised."

I imagined this snow scene at Parson Woodforde's church at Weston Longville. In 1793, he held the Christmas Day service and returned home with some of the village poor to have "boiled rabbit and onion sauce, surloin of beef roasted, plump puddings and mince pies"

Andrew Dodds

After the frolic Woodforde, with £250 or more of tithes in hand, would settle his accounts. About the middle of December, he would ride the nine miles of winding country road into Norwich, put up at the King's Head, on Gentleman's Walk, and then go out to settle with his attorney, his wine merchant, his tailor, his wig-maker, Nancy's mantua maker, and the rest of the city tradesmen with whom he dealt. This was a sociable excursion, for to people like Priest the wine merchant, Woodforde was a friend as well as a customer.

Between then and Christmas there were exchanges of visits and dinners, between Woodforde and his old friends. On December 21, St Thomas's Day, it was customary for the poor of the parish to walk round to the houses of the well-to-do for "something against Christmas," and year after year Woodforde notes that he gave them sixpence each, the total being usually something over £1. Dear Old Woodforde! It is more cheerful to leave him there, in the 1780s and in the midst of his hearty middle age, than to go on to the last volume of the diary, where he is still struggling to keep up the old customs, but tormented by indigestion and gout, and sorely pinched by the winds and frosts of a series of hard winters. He was no saint, but he was a delightful character.

Eric Fowler (*Jonathan Mardle*) *Eastern Daily Press*.
Reprinted 19 December 2000

Parson James Woodforde died on New Year's Day 1803.

It would be impossible to compile any anthology about Norfolk and not include something on Nelson, for North Norfolk is *Nelson Country*.

The Norfolk Hero: Vice-Admiral Horatio, Lord Nelson

Horatio Nelson was born on 29 September 1758 at Burnham Thorpe where his father was rector. As with many great men stories of his early signs of future courage probably owe more to sentiment and hindsight than they do to historical accuracy. In James Hooper's book *Nelson's Homeland*, published in 1905, a story of boyhood courage in the snow is repeated and the frontispiece illustration to Edmund Sellar's *The Story of Nelson*, in *The Children's Heroes Series,* shows boy and pony struggling through deep snow with a windmill in the background:

One Christmas Eve he laid a wager that, despite a snowstorm that was raging, he would go within a given time from the rectory to the churchyard and back again, bearing evidence of the accomplishment of his task by bringing a sprig from a low, bushy yew tree (which yet stands and bears berry) that grew on the south side of the church near the tower. The churchyard was at some distance, and the surroundings were dreary and far from the road. As the time in which he ought to have returned was far exceeded, his relatives grew anxious, and went in search of him. It was well that they did so, for he had sunk into deep snow, and had he not been rescued would have lost his life.

James Hooper - Nelson's Homeland. 1905

Nelson's father, the Reverend Edmund Nelson, had been married to Catherine Suckling, of Barsham in Suffolk, in Saint Michael's Church, Beccles, and it was Catherine's brother, Captain Maurice Suckling, who fulfilled young Horatio's dream of going to sea:

During the Christmas holidays of 1770-71, while their father was taking his annual "recruit" at Bath, William and Horace read in a local newspaper that the *Raisonnable*, of 64 guns, was being recommissioned in view of war with Spain. She had been captured from the French twelve years past, and, like most captured ships taken into the English service, had retained her old name. The appointment of her Captain was presented as likely to be of interest to Norfolk readers - Captain Maurice Suckling of Woodton. Their naval uncle was the most romantic figure in the boys' world...

To read in a newspaper that their uncle, who had been on half-pay for some time, was going to sea again, and with a prospect of active service, was naturally of intense interest to the boys of Burnham Thorpe Parsonage. To Horace the paragraph suggested something further: "Do, brother William, write to my father at Bath, and tell him I should like to go with my uncle Maurice to sea." William obediently wrote, and the Rector, who was in weak health and still had seven children to place, passed on the request, and in due time came a hearty answer from a surprised sea-officer: "What has poor Horace done, who is so weak, that he above all the rest should be sent to rough it out at sea? But let him come; and the first time we go into action, a cannon-ball may knock off his head, and provide for him at once."

Horatio Nelson was rated on the books of the *Raisonnable* as midshipman, from January 1, 1771. He was twelve years and three months old...

Carola Oman. *Nelson* – Reprinted 1996

Nelson's career in the Navy had begun.

Parson Woodforde's diary is still in print and available in a number of editions, scholarly, illustrated and paperback, but another clerical diarist's writings are out of print and no longer easy to find in secondhand book shops:

The Reverend Benjamin Armstrong of Dereham

The Reverend Benjamin Armstrong (1817-1890) reveals a great deal about Victorian Norfolk, particularly East Dereham, in his diaries. He became vicar of the church of Saint Nicholas at Dereham in 1850 and held the living until ill health forced him to retire in 1888.

Armstrong's Norfolk was criss-crossed by railway lines and day trips to London were possible. He recorded abnormally mild or severe weather, snowdrifts, floods, foot-and-mouth disease, Lord Hastings's hounds meeting at Elsing Hall, frequent problems with the bellringers, the annual choir suppers at the King's Arms, his sixty-six-year-old organist marrying a twenty-eight-year-old bride, going to the circus at Norwich, attending the opening of Gressenhall Union's new chapel, the first church heating and meetings with a clerical near-neighbour, Augustus Jessop, Rector of Scarning and previously headmaster of Norwich Grammar School.

He mentions events of national importance, including the death of the Prince Consort, the Prince of Wales purchasing the estate of Sandringham and being dangerously ill there a few years later, the Zulu War and the Tay Bridge disaster.

Reverend Armstrong died a few days before Christmas 1890 and is buried, with his wife and two daughters, who died before him, in the churchyard at Dereham.

The Man Who Wrote *King Solomon's Mines*

Henry Rider Haggard (1856-1925) grew up at Bradenham Hall, and later recalled the Christmases of his childhood there with affection, but his travels took him to Africa and gave him the background material for his highly successful adventure novels. *King Solomon's Mines* made his name as a writer of exotic adventures.

He moved to Ditchingham House when he married and ran the Ditchingham estate as a working farm. This was a time of agricultural depression when cheap food could be imported from around the world. In 1916 he abandoned farming.

Rider Haggard left two books containing detailed descriptions of Christmas preparations and festivities. He describes, day-by-day, his farming activities in 1898 and his gardening work in 1903. His gardening schemes were supported by a number of skilled staff unimaginable to professional gardeners today:

A Farmer's Year

As I write, the fear takes me that such a journal as I propose of agricultural and countryside events, and of reflections arising out of them, may prove monotonous; but if so, doubtless it will be my skill that is to seek, since nature is never monotonous... But if my artless tale is dull, I trust that to some extent it may prove useful to those who are weary of text-books and yet wish to learn something about rural ways and life upon the land in this era of dreadful depression, when the fate of British agriculture hangs quivering in the balance...

January 1, 1898. - Never within my recollection have we experienced so mild and open a winter as that of the year which died yesterday. There has been no rain, and until the 24th of last month, when it froze for a few hours, practically no frost, nor in my recollection has the land for a single day been too hard or too wet to plough. Christmas Day, with one exception, was the most beautiful that I can remember in this country. That exception was a certain Christmas five or six and twenty years gone, which I spent at my father's house in another part of Norfolk. There had been a heavy snowfall during the preceding night, followed by frost, so that in the morning the snow lay inches thick upon the fir-boughs, bending them down in deep arches till they almost touched the earth, while the sun shone upon the glittering surface of the white world till the eyes ached to look at it. One often hears of a mad hare, but this long dead Christmas Day was the only occasion upon which I ever saw one, for I recollect that as we were walking to church we perceived a hare tearing round and round in a circle through the snow in a neighbouring field. Being young in those days, of course I went to catch it, and succeeded. On examination the creature showed no sign of having been shot or otherwise injured, so I can only suppose that it was suffering from some sort of a fit.

This last Christmas Day differed from that which I have described, since there was no snow and only a few degrees of frost. But after its own fashion it was as beautiful, for in the morning every branchlet of the trees showed thick with a wonderful white rime, more perfect than any I have seen of late, because of the extraordinary calmness of the air. By the time that we came out of church this rime had melted in the bright sunshine, but the day remained frosty and windless. The best part of it, however, was the sunset as seen from the Bungay Road – a huge ball of fire that vanished gradually behind a deep background of spreading wreaths of vapour, smoky red in hue, roll upon roll of them covering the western sky. Against this sombre and glorious pall the trees in the foreground stood out nakedly, every bough, and indeed each separate twig, outlined and accentuated with fire, as in the morning they had been outlined and accentuated by frost. Then, to complete the picture, in the clear blue-black of the heavens above hung the crescent moon. Altogether it was an evening to be remembered.

That night promised sharper cold, but the promise was not to be fulfilled, for on Sunday the 26th the frost began to break and the moon came ringed into a clear sky. Moreover, I heard curlew calling over Bungay Common - it is impossible for anyone who knows it to mistake that wild and melancholy note, although I cannot recall hearing it here before. This I took as a sign of bad weather; nor was I wrong, for on the morrow the frost had departed and half a gale blew from the sou'-west, which on the 30th developed into a full gale. But like some worn-out old man, the year died quietly…

As the old year died so the new year was born, in peace and beauty, a mild southerly wind barely stirring the black trees…

To-day two carts are carrying refuse from the undrained town of Bungay to be scattered on that part of the nine acres of land…which is coming for root, or on so much of it as we can spare time and horses to cover. We have been at the task for nearly a week, sometimes with two and sometimes with three carts, and, I think, have spread about fifty loads upon the root land. This compost, disagreeable as it is in many ways and mixed with troublesome stuff, such as old tins and broken glass, is the best manure which I have ever used; but I think that to get its full value it should be spread upon the land and ploughed in at once, leaving it to decompose beneath the surface. I adopted this plan last year on the piece of rootland at All Hallows Farm…and with the most excellent results. The field is small, but, notwithstanding the drought, the piece of beet which resulted was the finest that I have yet grown. The cost of this manure is about two shillings the load as it lies upon the heap, and I suppose that the carting would come to as much more. Against this expense, however, it must be remembered that it spares the farmyard, upon which the calls are heavy and continuous; also for a root crop I would rather use it than any expensive artificial dressing on the market.

December

Many men come to know each other at shooting parties who, although near neighbours, otherwise would remain strangers all their lives. Also as a by-product it provides an enormous supply of cheap food for the dwellers in towns. These, together with the healthiness of the recreation, are some of the advantages of the sport; indeed, to my mind its only disadvantage is that it involves the necessity of putting a large number of creatures to a death which is sometimes lingering. Personally I salve my conscience - or try to - with the thought that were they not destined to be shot, they would never live at all, and that until they are shot their fortunes are excellent. Do away with shooting and in twenty years scarcely a game-bird would exist in England, except such of them as stress of weather or the instinct of migration might drive upon our shores.

The shortest day has passed. Nature, her despair outworn, turns her face again towards light and life. Little wonder that our Norse ancestors made a great Yule feast to celebrate the birth of the new season - the season of the lengthening days and kindling sun.

Christmas Day. - Upon the 22nd fell the first frost of the year, which rendered the land so hard that on the following day the ploughs could only just manage to get through with the work of breaking up the stubble land, as ploughing for crop was out of the question...

My correspondence to-day contains a letter from that rare person, an agricultural enthusiast. This gentleman, who is earning a very handsome salary in an office, proposes to abandon it in order to commence farming, apparently on borrowed capital. And what, my reader, do you suppose has led him to his resolve? No, not the earlier pages of a certain book, but – *the teachings of Carlyle and Ruskin.* If a study of these leaders of thought tends to such amiable insanity, which I confess has never struck me in reading them, surely so far as the young are concerned, they should be placed upon the *Index Expurgatorius.*

I have written imploring my correspondent to forsake these false lights and stick to his safe and gilded stool...

Royal Duke, the prize ox, made his last appearance at Ditchingham this evening in the shape of sirloin of beef. The meeting was painful to me who had known him from a calf, but I must admit that he was excellent eating. Oh! What carnivoræ we are!

Yesterday the frost broke, with the result that this Christmas has not the beauty of that of last year... In the afternoon I went to hear some carols sung in the neighbouring church of Broome. Afterwards a friend of mine, who lives there, gave me some curious facts illustrative of the decrease of population in that parish. It is his habit to make a present of meat at Christmas to every cottage inhabitant of Broome, and he informed me that the difference in its cost owing to the shrinkage of population between this year and last is something really remarkable.

I wonder what must be the result of this exodus if it continues? Will the most of the land have to be put down in temporary pasture and cultivated more roughly?... I have a friend connected with Argentina who tells me that a frozen meat company in which he is a shareholder is able to sell excellent chilled mutton at twopence-halfpenny the pound.

How are British graziers to compete against mutton at twopence-halfpenny a pound?

H. Rider Haggard - Abridged from *A Farmer's Year: Being his Commonplace Book for 1898.* 1899

They timed their rail journey from Thetford via Norwich to King's Lynn so that they reached the royal station in mid-afternoon, when a car took them to Sandringham.   *Mr America (Eastern Daily Press)*

While he was Prince of Wales, Queen Victoria's son, Edward, bought Sandringham, in the west of the county, as a sporting estate. He entertained many royal and aristocratic guests there over the years, and some who were less aristocratic, but none of his real-life guests could have been as troublesome as the fictional General Flashman:

Christmas 1909: Flashman at Sandringham

The visit when it came proved to be no ordeal at all... Thanks to Samson, they timed their rail journey from Thetford via Norwich to King's Lynn so that they reached the royal station in mid-afternoon, when a car took them to Sandringham. It was much more modest than Mr Franklin had imagined, and he tasted the informality of the place within a minute of his arrival. As he stood in the pleasant, light-panelled hall waiting to be shown his room, a high-pitched female voice from the open drawing-room instructed the footman to show him in directly, and he found himself in the presence of a most elegant, elderly lady who, with another younger lady, was engrossed in a jigsaw puzzle; without introduction they demanded his assistance, and it was only when he tentatively suggested fitting a piece of cloud into a piece of sky, and realized that the elegant lady was extremely deaf, that it dawned on him that he was doing a jigsaw puzzle with the Queen, with his travelling-cape still over his shoulders and his hat in his hand.

An imperturbable butler presently arrived and belatedly announced him; Mr Franklin made his bow with his piece of cloud poised to fit into place, the Queen rewarded him with a dazzling smile and informed him that the puzzle was a birthday gift from a grandchild, and he was then permitted to escape under the butler's wing, feeling a trifle dazed. In his room he confided to Samson, who was laying out his new subdued herring-bone tweed for tea, that at least the visit had got off to a good start; Samson, who had already undertaken a backstairs scouting operation of his own, briefed his employer on the composition of the house-party.

"Quite small, sir. Their majesties, Mr and Mrs Keppel, the Marquis of Soveral, and one or two others whom you know. The Marquess of Ivegill and his daughter, who was a lady-in-waiting to the Princess of Wales..."

Mr Franklin, who was human enough still to be contemplating jigsaws and the charming condescension of royalty, heard him with half his attention, and presently, at a quarter to five, made his way downstairs to the drawing room, marvelling at the number of framed photographs which seemed to cover small tables in every nook and cranny along the way. Sandringham was a remarkably cosy, family sort of place, it seemed to him; even so, he approached the drawing-room cautiously...

It was embarrassing; there appeared to be no one else in the drawing-room, and he was wondering if he should withdraw and come back later when he became aware of volcanic noises from a deep leather arm-chair half-hidden by a large Chinese screen. There was the sound of a newspaper being violently crumpled, a creaking of springs, and elderly arthritic gasps, and then a man emerged from behind the screen. He was extremely old and extremely large; Mr Franklin had an impression of stalwart height, and massive shoulders encased in a beautifully-cut frock coat of antique design, with a flower in its button-hole; above, reared a striking head of silver hair framing a lined, mottled face half-concealed by magnificent flowing white whiskers. It was the face of an aged, inebriated satyr, with a prominent heavily-veined nose and dark, bloodshot eyes... The old gentleman fixed a wicked eye on Mr Franklin... "Don't know you, do I?"

Mr Franklin admitted it, and introduced himself.

"American, eh? Well, well, now." The old gentleman drew himself
up and looked Mr Franklin over with interest. "Where from?
Nebraska, eh? My stars, how long is it since I was in Omaha?
Thirty-odd years, anyway. Changed, I expect. Know Kansas, do
you? No?" The old man chuckled and shook his head, fingering his
flowing whiskers. "I was a deputy marshal there, in Abilene, years
ago. Before you were born. What d'ye think of that?..." And the old
gentleman gestured impatiently and stood aside to admit the
American to the space behind the screen... "My dear, may I present
Mr Franklin, of Nebraska, U.S.A. - my great-niece, Lady Helen
Cessford."

To Mr Franklin's surprise, there was a lady sitting on a chaise-longue
beside the window; she glanced up with a cool smile, and then stared;
Mr Franklin, in the act of bowing, stopped and stared also. The old
gentleman, his glittering, blood-shot eye darting from one to other of
them, cocked his head.
"Met before, have you?"
Mr Franklin hesitated. He would have recognized that face
anywhere, with its broad white brow and proud lines; the rather long
nose and generous mouth, the imperious hazel eyes appraising him
coldly. The last time - indeed, the only time - he had met their owner,
she had been selling a suffragette magazine outside the Waldorf
Hotel, and doing her best to get arrested. And now, here she was, in
the King's drawing-room...

"What d'you say, Franklin? You approve of votes for our fair sex -
give 'em equal say with men in the running of the country?"

Mr Franklin smiled and shook his head. "I'd rather not be drawn
into any arguments, sir, if you don't mind. The last one didn't end
too happily, and if I may I'd like to take this opportunity of
apologizing to - "

Lady Helen rose abruptly to her feet. "If you will excuse me. I think tea is about to be served.".… With two graceful steps Lady Helen disappeared round the screen, and Uncle Harry shook his great head reproachfully at Mr Franklin.

"You don't know much, do you? Never apologize to 'em in public. Especially when they're like Helen - proud as Lucifer and dam' contrary. She'll make some poor devil the deuce of a wife one of these days. Fine gal, mind you, dam' fine. Reminds me of a female I knew in Russia – oh, years ago, in the Crimea. Sara, her name was. Partial to steam-baths. Got me into no end of bother. Button - Helen – is like that, too. Born to trouble as the sparks fly upward. Got her head full of this suffragette nonsense - well, I don't care, women are as fit to vote as men, any day, for my money. That's why I bailed her out – because she's got ten times the spirit of these other mealy little nursery tarts…"

"Mind you, I don't think any the less of her for it, and if I haven't boozed all my fortune away by the time I kick the bucket, she'll get her share. Any woman with a figure like that deserves well, although I'm her own grand-uncle that says it. Mind you, they're hell, these good-looking gals with strong characters; you must watch out for them. Take your own country," he went on, settling himself comfortably. "American women are the frozen limit. I remember one - black gal, she was…escaped slave, can't think of her name offhand…deuce of a dance she led me. Beautiful, but with a will of iron. I got shot in the backside over her, which goes to show you…"

"I believe they're having tea," said Mr Franklin. "Perhaps we should –"

"Let 'em! To hell with 'em!" was the rejoinder. "You don't want to go out there, surely? You'll have to talk to that bounder Bertie - " Mr Franklin winced at this indiscreetly loud reference to his majesty " – and eat their vile sandwiches, and stand around like Lord Fauntleroy. Ghastly!" Uncle Harry shuddered at the thought. "Is the Keppel wench there? Fine buttocks she's got. But - tea! I'm eighty-eight next May, and I attribute my longevity to an almost total abstinence from tea..."

The course of tea-time conversation moved Mr Franklin from group to group; he chatted with the Queen and Soveral, joked about bridge with Mrs Keppel, and finally worked his way to where Lady Helen was presiding at one of the twin silver tea services...
"I like your great-uncle... You must be very proud of him, I should think."
"Extremely," said Lady Helen, and at that moment another guest arrived for tea...

He had enough male vanity, of course, to tell himself that that was not the end of the matter. Some men retire permanently chilled before personalities like Lady Helen Cessford's; others, and Mr Franklin was discovering that he was one of them, merely have their interest piqued; he found himself hoping that she might be placed beside him at dinner, and was disappointed when his partners turned out to be a perfectly charming lady-in-waiting and a most affable Jewish knight... Lady Helen was placed near the foot of the table, plainly to keep an eye on her eccentric great-uncle, who had been removed as far from the King as was possible. He sat glittering-eyed, like an elderly and debauched eagle, imbibing heroic quantities of champagne without visible effect...

To Mr Franklin the most interesting thing about the meal was the contrast with the last dinner he had had with royalty... Here the King was on his home ground; there was no question of hosts and hostesses falling over themselves to please, or communicating their nervousness to him when things went wrong... At Sandringham he was completely at ease, content in the company of people he knew and (General Flashman excepted) liked; if he didn't care for the fish he could say so, without having to feel that he was voicing a complaint that would be recalled with shame for a lifetime; everyone knew him and all his foibles, and there would be no gaffes to throw a pall of embarrassment over the company. It was cosy, and happy, and he could enjoy himself in the certainty that his guests were enjoying themselves, too...

In the morning there was a pheasant shoot, which occupied most of the daylight hours...

Home the day after tomorrow...thought Mr Franklin, and in the meantime we'll break the monotony by a spirited chat with Lady Helen on the subject of women's rights, or the provocation of policemen, and see if there isn't a more amiable side to her after all.

But in this he was disappointed. When the party returned to the house it was discovered that she and her great-uncle had left unexpectedly. General Flashman, excused the shooting party on the score of his age and presumed infirmity, had belied the latter by beguiling the time indoors with sporting activities of his own. These had included a late breakfast of champagne mixed with brandy, and the pursuit of a personable young between-stairs maid to whom, by report, he had offered the most enthusiastic familiarities. The maid, a nimble girl, had escaped by a short head, but the old warrior's ardent advance had resulted in his losing his footing at the head of the stairs, colliding with a table loaded with photographs of Queen Victoria's German nieces, and coming to rest in the hall with a sprained ankle. In the circumstances his great-niece had thought it best to remove him, and he had been borne protesting to a motor car which had carried them both to King's Lynn. None of which was referred to publicly, of course, the official version being that the General had had one of his feverish turns again - which was true enough, in its way...

George MacDonald Fraser - Abridged from *Mr American.* 1980

Happisburgh Lifeboat

24 December 1910

The *Jacob and Rachel Valentine* lifeboat from Happisburgh, which had been dedicated in 1907, was launched for the first time to the barquentine *Scotia*, of Folkestone, bound from London to Hartlepool. The vessel was stranded and leaking, but she was refloated with the assistance of the lifeboat and a tug.

Nicholas Leach - *The Happisburgh Lifeboats.* 1999

December 22nd 1957 – Listened to *Scrapbook for 1914*, ending with the fraternisation in No-Man's-Land on Christmas Day. One felt what a turning point it might have been in history if the whole of the two armies had thrown down their arms and shaken hands....

Adrian Bell 4 January 1958 *The Spiral Stair*

I had read several times of this unofficial truce held at Christmas in the trenches of France in World War I, but I had found no account of the event written at first hand. Then I bought a copy of Henry Williamson's *The Story of a Norfolk Farm* and discovered that the author of *Tarka the Otter* had been one of the men who had set his rifle aside at Christmas in 1914:

42

A Vision of Christmas: Christmas 1914

Christmas Eve, 1937

It is Christmas again, and I have a rendezvous in ancient moonlight, with you and you and you, unknown comrades of that first Christmas…when for myself and my friends, a miracle broke into the near-hopelessness of our youthful lives… A long time ago, Christmas 1914… Yet we still hope, those who were there - the living and the dead - that the vision of peace we *lived* during those few rare hours may be made real and everlasting.

The cries of the wild geese bring sharply before me a bare and frozen wood of Flanders, charcoal braziers, bearded men in woollen balaclava helmets, rifles piled, starlight, and the smoke of green wood fires.

On Christmas Eve of 1914 we were in the support line, about two hundred yards inside Ploegsteert Wood. It was freezing. Our overcoats were stiff as boards, our boots were too hard to remove, but we rejoiced. The mud was hard too! Also, happy thought, we would be able to *sleep* that night - inside a new blockhouse of oak-boughs and sandbags called Piccadilly Hotel. No bed but the cold earth, no blankets even; but sleep. Sleep!

We heard singing from the German lines - carols the tunes of which we knew. I noticed a very bright light on a tall pole, raised in their lines. Down opposite the East Lancs trench, in front of the convent, a Christmas tree, with lighted candles, was set on their parapet… Cries of 'Come over, Tommy! We won't fire at you!'

A dark figure approached me, hesitatingly. A trap? I walked towards it, with bumping heart. 'Merry Christmas, English friend!' We shook hands, tremulously. Then I saw that the light on the pole was the Morning Star, the Star in the East. It was Christmas morning.

All Christmas Day grey and khaki figures mingled and talked in no-man's-land. Picks and spades rang in the hard ground. It was strange to stare at the dead we had only glimpsed, swiftly, from the trenches. The shallowest graves were dug, filled, and set with crosses knocked together from lengths of ration-box wood, marked with indelible pencil. 'For King and Country.' 'Für Vaterland und Freiheit.'

A most shaking, staggering thought: that both sides thought they were fighting for the same cause! The war was a terrible mistake! People at home did not know this! Then the Idea came to the young and callow soldier, that if only he could tell them all at home *what was really happening*, and if the German soldiers told their people the truth about us, the war would be over. But he hardly dared to think it, even to himself.

The next day was quiet, and the next. Waving hands from the trenches by day; singing and reflected blaze of trench bonfires at night. It was a lovely time...

Two days later, an Army Order came from G.H.Q. to the effect that men found fraternizing with the enemy would be court-martialled, and if found guilty, would suffer the death penalty.

So Hope sank into the mud again...

Henry Williamson - Abridged from *The Story of a Norfolk Farm*. 1941

There is another, of whom I am aware on the brink of another year, who dared to cry, "Patriotism is not enough"... Just a nurse; who had heard of her? But her death gave birth to four imperishable words...

Adrian Bell 4 January 1958 *The Spiral Stair*

Adrian Bell (1901-1980) was born in Manchester and grew up in London. He worked as a farm pupil in Suffolk, close to where Highpoint Prison now stands, and then farmed in the west and east of the county before becoming a full-time writer. His *Countryman's Notebook* essays appeared in the *Eastern Daily Press* every Saturday for thirty years. He lived in Redisham, Beccles and Barsham, but spent the last few months of his life on the northern side of the River Waveney at Gillingham:

A Sprig of Holly: Christmas 1918

After a certain age one looks askance at birthdays, but Christmas Days are always welcome...

The year was 1918. London was still in a state of slightly hysterical reaction from the Great War. My father was absent. Why was he not with us at the pantomime? He had always taken us to the Kennington Pantomime when we lived at Streatham.

But he distributed tickets for the first post-war pantomime - the full dress rehearsal of the Drury Lane show on Christmas Eve.

It was a mammoth production. It went on and on... I was ceasing to enjoy this pantomime, and was wishing it would stop. But it would not stop.

We were late - long past brother's and sister's bedtime, and a long train journey before us by underground and puffer back to Enfield. My brother's hilarity had turned to furious complaint at being dragged away. Sister just crumpled up and slept.

It was one hour to Christmas Day, 1918. We went up in the lift from the underground at King's Cross. Only two railmen going off duty shared the lift with us. It stopped, the door slid open. They paused a moment before parting. "Well, all the best, mate," said one. "All the best," replied the other.

An essential part of the Christmas of our schooldays. Mulbarton School's Nativity play in 1965.

Eastern Daily Press

I have never forgotten that moment, which had nothing to make it remembered. Elsewhere, cathedrals coruscated, midnight mass approached its climax, bells were poised to peal. But here was only the exhausted midnight of a London terminus, and one small sprig of holly which one man had stuck in his uniform cap, as he braced himself against the inrush of cold air, and stepped out hopefully into that Peace which we now call "between the Wars."

"All the best, mate."

"All the best."

Adrian Bell - Abridged from *A Countryman's Notebook.*
24 December 1966

Robert Bagshaw grew up in North Walsham. He writes of his happy childhood and recollects in this passage that not all the drama in the life of the mixed infants' class took place on the stage:

The Sad Tale of Humpty Dumpty

My early years at the Council School had not brought me into contact with Mr Colthorpe, for I started there at the age of five and was classed as a "mixed infant". It is true that he was head of the entire school, but he rarely gave his attention to us, preferring to leave us in the tender care of Miss Gow and Miss Dennis.

Miss Gow was, I suppose, a typical country schoolteacher. She was of uncertain age and there was nothing about her, either physically or academically, which would have made her stand out in a crowd. She was, however, a mother to us all, and her mode of discipline was based on love and respect rather than on fear.

She was assisted in her ministrations by Miss Dennis. Now, Miss Dennis was a different matter altogether. She was young and pretty, and when she smiled at me my legs turned to jelly. I loved Miss Dennis very much.

The most exciting period of the year in the Infants' School was, of course, the few weeks before Christmas. Then it was that the increasing excitement of the coming celebration was heightened by the frantic activity which was necessary to make sure that everything would be ready on time. Little brushes were dipped into gluepots and applied to strips of paper, which then became transformed into multicoloured chains to decorate the classroom walls. Crêpe paper was cut and, with a combination of dexterity and pins, became gaudy balls to hang from any available hook. Christmas cards, of an extreme simplicity matched only by their childish sincerity, were churned out ready for distribution to mothers and fathers, aunts and uncles, with an extra two being made in secret for Miss Gow and Miss Dennis.

But, above all, there was much work to be done in preparation for the annual school concert. This, of course, was no different from any other infants' concert, but to us it was an event of the greatest magnitude. The first time I took part in one of these productions was also the first time I had appeared on a public stage, and I was five years old. It was the conventional nativity story and I was to play the part of an owl. Looking back, I become aware that it was the only time I have ever known an owl to take part in a nativity play. I strongly suspect that the part was written in specially for me! Anyway, I was to be swathed in a piece of fur and put in my position behind a papier-mâché tree, on the branch of which I was supposed to be perched. Then, as Joseph and Mary trudged on stage on their way to Bethlehem, I was to utter those immortal lines, "Tu-whit, to-whoo; tu-whit, to-whoo; tu-whit, to-whoo." I rehearsed with all the dedication of a National Theatre player and my début went like a dream. Like every children's nativity play that has ever been presented, the show was a great success.

The Infants' Concert of the following year, though again voted a hit by the general public, was, for me, a personal disaster. This time we were performing a piece involving a selection of nursery rhyme characters and I was to play Humpty Dumpty. I was never under-weight as a child, but I still needed much help to create the image of the part, so our teachers set to work and made a most complicated cardboard frame which covered me from neck to ankles. The result was most impressive. There was this massive cardboard ostrich egg with my little head peeping out of the top and a pair of tiny feet underneath. I was unable to walk when I had the costume on, and Miss Dennis had to lift me on to the stage. I enjoyed that part most of all!

Well, all went well until the day of the Dress Rehearsal. I was feeling distinctly unwell that day and, by the time we had been taken to the Church Rooms to go through our parts, I was decidedly groggy. Miss Gow came to have a look at me and declared that I was suffering from "swollen glands", but that I would feel better tomorrow. Her diagnosis was only partly correct. By the morning my "swollen glands" had become mumps and I was feeling infinitely worse. Needless to say, the show went on without Humpty Dumpty and I was in the depths of despair.

A few days later, however, my world brightened considerably, this transformation being brought about by three things. Firstly, I didn't feel ill any more. Secondly, I had the most wonderful swollen face which I was proud to show to anybody who might show an interest. But thirdly, and most important of all, a young messenger brought to our house a package for me which contained some sweets and a letter from the sender. The letter, which I treasure to this day, read:
> "Dear Bobby,
> This little box of sweets I hope you will enjoy. Perhaps
> it will make up a wee bit for your disappointment last

week. Trust you will soon be well enough to return to school.
Your loving teacher,
F. Gow."

Robert Bagshaw - *Poppies to Paston*. 1986

Dorothy L. Sayers (1893-1957), one of England's greatest writers of detective fiction, had strong family ties with Norfolk. I first read her novels, with their distinctive bright yellow Gollancz dust jackets, while I was at school. Dorothy Sayers' father was a clergyman and *The Nine Tailors*, with its Norfolk-based story of gruesome death and bellringing lore, is a book ideally suited to chilling the blood over Christmas and the New Year!

Considering her father's links with the parish of Upwell, it is not surprising that her fictional church at Fenchurch St. Paul shares at least one significant architectural feature with the church at Upwell:

Old Year's Night at Fenchurch St. Paul

"That's torn it!" said Lord Peter Wimsey.
The car lay, helpless and ridiculous, her nose deep in the ditch, her back wheels cocked absurdly up on the bank, as though she were doing her best to bolt to earth and were scraping herself a burrow beneath the drifted snow. Peering through a flurry of driving flakes, Wimsey saw how the accident had come about. The narrow, hump-backed bridge, blind as an eyeless beggar, spanned the dark drain at

right angles, dropping plump down upon the narrow road that crested the dyke. Coming a trifle too fast across the bridge, blinded by the bitter easterly snowstorm, he had overshot the road and plunged down the side of the dyke into the deep ditch beyond, where the black spikes of a thorn hedge stood bleak and unwelcoming in the glare of the headlights.

Right and left, before and behind, the fen lay shrouded. It was past four o'clock and New Year's Eve; the snow that had fallen all day gave back a glimmering greyness to a sky like lead.

"I'm sorry," said Wimsey. "Whereabouts do you suppose we've got to, Bunter?"

The manservant consulted a map in the ray of an electric torch.

"I think, my lord, we must have run off the proper road at Leamholt. Unless I am much mistaken, we must be near Fenchurch St. Paul."

As he spoke, the sound of a church clock, muffled by the snow, came borne upon the wind; it chimed the first quarter.

"Thank God!" said Wimsey. "Where there is a church, there is civilisation. We'll have to walk it. Never mind the suitcases; we can send somebody for them. Br'rh! it's cold... Next time I accept hospitality in the Fen-country, I'll take care that it's at mid-summer, or else I'll go by train. The church lies to windward of us, I fancy. It would."

They wrapped their coats about them and turned their faces to the wind and snow. To left of them, the drain ran straight as a rule could make it, black and sullen, with a steep bank shelving down to its slow, unforgiving waters... They tramped on in silence, the snow beating on their eyelids. At the end of a solitary mile the gaunt shape of a windmill loomed up upon the farther bank of the drain, but no bridge

51

led to it, and no light showed.

Another half-mile, and they came to a signpost and a secondary road that turned off to the right. Bunter turned his torch upon the signpost and read upon the single arm: "Fenchurch St. Paul."

There was no other direction; ahead, road and dyke marched on side by side into an eternity of winter.

"Fenchurch St. Paul for us," said Wimsey. He led the way into the side-road, and as he did so, they heard the clock again - nearer - chiming the third quarter.

A few hundred yards of solitude, and they came upon the first sign of life in this frozen desolation: on their left, the roofs of a farm, standing some way back from the road, and, on the right, a small, square building like a box of bricks, whose sign, creaking in the blast, proclaimed it to be the Wheatsheaf public-house. In front of it stood a small, shabby car, and from windows on the ground and first floors light shone behind red blinds.

Wimsey went up to it and tried the door. It was shut, but not locked. He called out, "Anybody about?"
A middle-aged woman emerged from an inner room.
"We're not open yet," she began, abruptly.
"I beg your pardon," said Wimsey. "Our car has come to grief. Can you direct us…?"
"Oh, I'm sorry, sir. I thought you were some of the men. Your car broke down? That's bad. Come in. I'm afraid we're all in a muddle…"

"What's the trouble, Mrs Tebbutt?" The voice was gentle and scholarly, and, as Wimsey followed the woman into a small parlour, he saw that the speaker was an elderly parson.
"The gentlemen have had an accident with their car."

"Oh dear," said the clergyman. "Such a terrible day, too! Can I be of any assistance?"

Wimsey explained that the car was in the ditch, and would certainly need ropes and haulage to get it back to the road again.

"Dear, dear," said the clergyman again. "That would be coming over Frog's Bridge, I expect. A most dangerous place, especially in the dark. We must see what can be done about it. Let me give you a lift into the village."
"It's very good of you, sir."
"Not at all, not at all. I am just getting back to my tea. I am sure you must be wanting something to warm you up. I trust you are not in a hurry to reach your destination. We should be delighted to put you up for the night."

Wimsey thanked him very much, but said he did not want to trespass upon his hospitality.

"It will be a great pleasure," said the clergyman, courteously. "We see so little company here that I assure you you will be doing my wife and myself a great favour."
"In that case..." said Wimsey.
"Excellent, excellent."
"I'm really most grateful. Even if we could get the car out tonight, I'm afraid the axle may be bent, and that means a blacksmith's job..."

"Dear me! Well! We really must be going. I'm afraid my car is not much to boast of, but there's more room in it than one would think... ...Will you sit beside me, Lord Peter? Your man and your - dear me! have you any luggage?... Ah! Down at Frog's Bridge? I will send my gardener to fetch it. It will be quite safe where it is; we're all honest people about here, aren't we, Mrs. Tebbutt?"

The ancient car, shuddering to her marrow-bones, lurched away down the straight and narrow road. They passed a cottage, and then, quite suddenly, on their right, there loomed out of the whirling snow a grey, gigantic bulk.

"Great Heavens!" exclaimed Wimsey, "is that your church?"

"Yes, indeed," said the Rector, with pride. "You find it impressive?"

"Impressive!" said Wimsey. "Why, it's like a young cathedral. I'd no idea. How big is your parish, then?"

"You'll be surprised when I tell you," said the Rector, with a chuckle. "Three hundred and forty souls - no more. Astonishing, is it not? But you find the same thing all over the Fens. East Anglia is famous for the size and splendour of its parish churches. Still, we flatter ourselves we are almost unique, even in this part of the world. It was an abbey foundation, and in the old days Fenchurch St. Paul must have been quite an important place. How high should you say our tower was?"

Wimsey gazed up at the great pile.

"It's difficult to tell in this darkness. Not less than a hundred and thirty feet, surely."

"Not a bad guess. A hundred and twenty-eight, to be exact, to the top of the pinnacles, but it looks more, because of the comparative lowness of the clerestory roof. There aren't many to beat us. St. Peter Mancroft, of course - but that's a town church. And St. Michael's, Coventry is one hundred and thirty feet without the spire. But I would venture to back Fenchurch St. Paul against them all for beauty of proportion…"

Dorothy Sayers - Abridged from *The Nine Tailors.* 1934

The Worst Trip that Henry Blogg Ever Made

Christmas week 1927 was a busy one for the lifeboat service... The Great Yarmouth and Gorleston boat went out four times on December 21. The storms did subside for a day or two, then on Christmas night they sprang up with added violence.

Henry Blogg of Cromer, photographed on the 18th March 1940 by the late P.A. Vicary.
Maritime Photo Library,
Cromer

Not only was the gale at full strength but with the wind came snow, piling into deep drifts that isolated many villages inland, and caused anxiety about supplies. Telegraph poles were blown down around the coast and communication was cut in many places...

While most of Cromer was enjoying the festivities behind stout walls, the men whose duty kept them from their own firesides, even on Christmas Day, were keeping anxious watch out to sea, for this gale had no goodwill for seamen. At 9 p.m. when the party fun was at its height, Haisbro' light-vessel reported disturbing news to the Cromer coastguard, and he in turn hastily consulted Henry Blogg. The s.s. *Crawford Castle* of the Union Castle Line, 2820 tons, in ballast, had been in collision with the light-vessel, and in view of the fierce east-north-east gale and exceptionally heavy seas the lifeboat might be needed at any moment.

At 10.15 p.m. the coastguard rang: the light-vessel had reported it had sustained slight damage in the collision. The steamer, however, was two miles to the north-west, and was showing 'out of control' lights. It appeared to be drifting towards shallow water.

Henry Blogg kept the crew at stand-by until 11.30 p.m., waiting...for the call that did not come. Just what was happening out there to the unmanageable ship in the storm they could not know, but they were not yet requested. As there was no further message it was decided to dismiss the crew, and the coastguard said he would let them know immediately there was any worsening of the situation.

It was not until 11.10 a.m. on that aptly named Boxing Day that action was required. The *Crawford Castle* was still out of control but was near the East Dudgeon light-vessel, thirty miles farther north. She was, however, now asking for lifeboat and tug assistance.

The maroons cracked and in almost record time the crew arrived. The *H.F. Bailey* was quickly launched into a terrific sea... That frightening start was the keynote of the whole voyage. Fortunately the lifeboat was the Watson-cabin type, for had it been an open boat like the famous Norfolk-and-Suffolk type, then the crew would have been washed right out of her as she plunged down the slipway into those rearing waves. Every man was soaked almost as soon as the boat was afloat.

George Balls, second coxswain, joined Henry Blogg at the helm to keep the boat steady in the seas that went right over them as they turned and headed north for the long run to the Dudgeon light-vessel.

The *H.F. Bailey* was not a quarter of a mile away from the slipway when a further message came through, passed on by the Haisbro' light-vessel, saying the steamer was under control and proceeding on its way. The coastguard immediately ran up the recall-signal, but so bad was the weather and thick the air with spindrift and spray that the crew never saw it, but kept on their way climbing the hills of green water and dipping into the valleys, standing at times almost on end, so steep were the waves.

The splendid boat battled every yard of the way with scuppers constantly working and icy spray and spume flying over her continuously. Every twenty minutes or so she took green seas on board, which completely buried her. The waves swept from end to end, filling the cockpit and causing every man to hang on grimly for life itself. The valves worked so efficiently, however, that the seas were rapidly cleared.

So, for mile after mile, the crew fought seas unparalleled in their experience, until they reached the position in which the steamer was expected. It could not be seen, so they began searching for a ship that, unbeknown to them, had gone on its way... Then the coxswain decided to talk to the light-vessel...and the master of the vessel reported that the steamer had nearly collided with him in the darkness before 6 a.m., and he had burned a couple of flares in warning. The *Crawford Castle* was apparently taking a tilt at light-vessels! He had last seen the ship going north under its own power about 10.30 a.m.

They had fought their way for thirty miles in the dirtiest weather they had known and in constant danger of being washed overboard, and now they were not needed.

There was nothing more they could do except get back home out of this bitter wind and berserk sea… In fact, the sea was so rough, and they had come so far north, that it was more practicable to carry on to Grimsby than to turn south for Cromer… Henry Blogg had never been in to Grimsby, nor had any of his crew. He had no chart of the coast, and it would soon be dark. To enter an unknown river-mouth without chart or pilot, in the dark, in those seas was a tremendous responsibility. The fact that Henry Blogg did it is a remarkable testimony to the man.

So they brought the bows of the *H.F. Bailey* round for the Humber. In his mind, as the boat climbed and dipped with the great seas lifting and leaving her, the coxswain tried to recall charts he had seen in a nautical almanac at home…

As darkness came the situation seemed so serious that the youngest members of the crew (there were three in their teens) were put in the most protected part of the boat, so that if the worst came to the worst and they were hit by one of these seas they would stand the best chance of surviving.

Back at Cromer the hours dragged by without news… Ann Blogg, perhaps because she had known so many anxious hours with her husband as coxswain, was a tower of strength… But Daniel Davison was so anxious that he organized a search-party, which set off in a car despite the gale. They drove along the Sheringham coast-road, searching the shore for the wreck of their lifeboat…. As the hours dragged by without news the earlier fears that the worst had happened seemed confirmed. The *H.F. Bailey* was missing.

The women just had to wait, resting on the assurance of the coastguard that as soon as he got any news he would let them know…

They then turned and went back to the house, perhaps to the children, to do mechanically, hour after hour, the ordinary jobs of the home with their minds all the time out on the waters with their loved one.

Theirs was the long, long wait and the gnawing anxiety...

The *H.F. Bailey* reached Grimsby about midnight. Somehow their incomparable coxswain had found the channel and brought them safely into harbour...utterly exhausted, yet safe, having survived sixty-five miles of the roughest voyage they had ever known.

Worn out, soaked and chilled to the marrow...the crew went ashore. They moored their boat and found the Sailors' Home in the dim-lit streets of the port. Stiff-limbed and sore, with eyes red and inflamed from the lashing of wind and sea, and salt glistening on skin and hair, they looked a bedraggled company. But if ever men had earned admiration they had. They had hot baths and were put into whatever dry clothes could be found for them. While they were doing this, Henry Blogg tried again and again to get through to Ann or the coastguard, but the lines were down. So the women had to wait all through that night until the next morning, when the crew...caught an early train at Grimsby. They changed at King's Lynn, and at last Henry Blogg managed to get a telephone message through from there. When they bought copies of the local paper they found the headline: "Cromer Lifeboat Missing."

When they got into the Midland and Great Northern Beach station they found a small crowd of friends and relatives to greet them, and the warmth of that reception told a lot of the crew just how much their families had endured while they had been away.

Cyril Jolly - Abridged from *Henry Blogg of Cromer*. 1958
Reprinted 2002 by Poppyland

Sir Peter Scott (1909-1989) is probably best remembered today for establishing the Wildfowl and Wetlands Trust at Slimbridge in Gloucestershire, but he also had strong connections with Norfolk. As an undergraduate at Cambridge he enjoyed wildfowling expeditions to the tidal marshes at Terrington St. Clement:

Peter Scott and *Kazarka*

I think it was Christopher Dalgety who first heard about the saltings at Terrington, to the west of King's Lynn. They were comparatively unknown to wildfowlers in those days. Michael and I went with him on the first exploration there. Christopher was the leader of the party. He was fair-haired and slight with a small fair moustache and a quick temper. No one could pour scorn more quickly or effectively on inefficiency. He did not suffer fools gladly and when you were foolish you were not suffered...

We kept the place darkly secret, inventing our own code name for it, 'Sandbanks', for it was only forty-four miles from Cambridge - an hour and a half's drive in Christopher's square-nosed Morris...

'Sandbanks' consisted then of a rough salting half a mile wide, bounded on the seaward side by mudflats, and on the landward side by a sea-wall protecting mile upon mile of flat neatly ditched fields. The salting was finely divided by a network of deep muddy creeks which branched and wriggled their way in from the sea... But the sky and the birds made it for me a place of incomparable beauty and romance...

During our Christmas holiday on the Solway we had heard rumours that very large numbers of geese assembled at the head of the great estuary upon their first arrival from the Arctic in late September...

For my last two days in Scotland I moved westward to Wigtown Bay in order to go punting with Major Hulse - the Expert as we called him. I joined him at Creetown and we spent the two days afloat in pursuit of wigeon, which confirmed my earlier conclusion that punting was the best that wildfowling had to offer...

After the two days' punting I set off from Creetown in the Austin Seven at a quarter to eight in the morning and arrived in London at a quarter to eight in the evening, having stopped for half an hour in Carlisle and three-quarters of an hour at Boroughbridge where I had lunch. It is an interesting commentary on the Great North Road and motoring conditions in 1929 that I was able to make the 380-mile journey in a seven-horsepower car at an average speed of just over 35 miles per hour. It is also perhaps worth recording that my ten days in Scotland had cost me almost exactly £10.

On the flood-waters of the Bedford Levels we had *Penelope* and *Grey Goose*, but we still had no sea-going double punt for the Wash, and this must clearly be remedied. Mr. Mathie, a boat-builder in Cambridge, was commissioned to build one, based mainly on the design and specifications of the Expert's punt. She was to be twenty-four foot long, four-foot beam, with a twelve-foot cockpit, and she was to be called *Kazarka* - the Russian name for the Red-breasted Goose.

Kazarka was launched just below Magdalene Bridge in Cambridge on 11th December, 1929. On the following day I set out with a companion, David Lewis, to sail her to the coast. There was a south-westerly wind which was very strong at times and we made good progress until just before Ely, when there was a stretch which came closer to the eye of the wind and the lee boards could not really cope with it. But a passing sugar beet tug took us in tow as far as the Ely beet factory. Thereafter we sailed without difficulty to Brandon

Creek which was to be our staging point for the day... The flat fenland fields, mostly below the level of the river, were hidden from us; and yet I remember that the passage, the testing of our boat on her maiden voyage, the anticipation of her arrival on the fowling grounds of the Wash, the pleasure of spinning along under the small sail, all added up to a sheer delight which I can clearly recall today - just thirty years later. Christopher Dalgety came to meet us at Brandon Creek, and we took David Lewis to Ely to catch a train (which he missed) and then went on to the Globe Hotel at King's Lynn which was our coastal headquarters.

Re-reading my shooting diaries in 1959 in the course of writing this book I came upon the entry for the following morning, Friday, 13th December, 1929...

When the morning flight was over at 'Skeldyke' (our new code name of Terrington Marsh since the old one - 'Sandbanks' - was already too widely known), we returned to breakfast at King's Lynn...and an hour later we were off to Brandon Creek to see that all was well with our new punt. It was, and that day we took her to Lynn. On the next she reached her anchorage in a big creek on Terrington Marsh. *Kazarka* was a better sea boat than we imagined, and we tested her several times. Here is one of them.

Monday, 23rd December, 1929 began badly. According to my diary "Christopher forgot the sandwiches which I left in his care." According to Christopher, as far as I can remember, I forgot the sandwiches which he had left in my care. It was a misty morning on 'Skeldyke' saltings and the geese were flying all over it, so that in spite of our bungling, and particularly of my bad marksmanship we bagged a Pinkfoot each and three Mallards and two Curlews as well. These we took back to the car and then set out for the punt. The mist had now cleared and our plan was to take *Kazarka* round into the River Nene four miles direct but three times as far by water at low tide, so as to leave her there while we all went home for Christmas...

It must have been noon by the time we reached the punt, to find her bridging the creek, supported only by the extreme stem and stern. However her back was not broken and we got her into the water only just in time, before the last of the tide went out of the bottom of the creek, leaving a narrow, winding and unnavigable trickle of water. In the course of the afternoon we made two rather small shots with the punt-gun…with the result that we had not done more than about a fifth of our journey by dusk…

The light was already beginning to fade and the S.S.E wind which had been freshening all day was now blowing really hard - also it had begun to drizzle, and we had had nothing to eat since 5.30 a.m. In the face of all this it was madness to attempt to go round into the Nene channel, which we did not know, on such a night. However, with neap tides we hoped to be able to cuff a good many corners… We set sail as quickly as possible and tore off down the 'eye', periodically touching the ground and nearly getting pooped by our own wake.
I think it was when we reached the end of this lead and had to jump out and pull the boat over a sand bar that we really began to realise our folly. Outside there was a big sea running, and it was nearly dark. Just as we ran into the sea I managed, with considerable effort, to get the big gun off the breeching ropes and bring it in board: then turning up the hinged coamings I just managed to get aft again before she burrowed. At each big wave she only just lifted clear with water pouring off the decks.

By the last of daylight we made out the corner and turned into a very shallow lead. We soon came on to a lee shore, for we had not got the lee boards out and she wouldn't make to windward at all. As soon as she was aground we got the sail down at once and tried to row. There was a shallow bar in front which we had to cross and we thought we had better hurry, as the tide was still falling. Rowing was no good, so we poled on to the bar - then jumped out and pulled the boat across. As soon as we were over Christopher got out the lee boards. He had some difficulty in putting them together, but eventually, after much swearing and hammering with the short pole, they were ready and he hoisted the sail. During this delay we had drifted some way down wind and we were also in deep water - over ten feet. However, we knew that if we sailed on a beam wind, after a mile of open water we must eventually reach the far bank of the Nene channel. If the wind veered there would be the lights of the fairway buoys outside in the Lynn channel behind us to give us direction. We could see them fairly well in spite of the rain. We were in deep water, however, and there were, of course, big waves. This was perhaps the nastiest moment. I found myself with a very dry mouth and I doubt if Christopher was any happier…

Diss Mere, Christmas 1971

Eastern Daily Press

After what seemed an age, during which the boat went well on a beam wind, and, all things considered, shipped comparatively little water, we decided that it was, nevertheless, about time to take off our rubber boots, and prepare to swim; but at that moment we thought we could see land ahead, and a minute or two later, with infinite relief, I touched bottom with the ten-foot pole. We ran ashore, and as it was obvious that we shouldn't want to sail any more (as our way lay into the wind), we stowed the mast and sail. Now, at any rate, we were safe, for we could leave the boat if necessary, and walk across the mud... The only way we decided was to walk and push the punt... However, so many waves were breaking in that it soon became obvious that the boat would sink unless something was done about it. So we arranged then that Christopher should tow in front with one of the breeching ropes walking in the water, whilst I sat on the stern and baled out the water as fast as it came in...

Then after about three-quarters of an hour of this the water got fairly suddenly calmer and we could see a bank opposite... Then we came to a dead end with shallow water all across. Over the sand on the east side we could hear the seas breaking, and we knew there was a channel there. ...All this time there were strange glows in the sky, some of which suddenly brightened and must have been cars on certain corners of the main road. They seemed incredibly close and comforting, but they must have been four miles away at the least. Other glows were from the towns - Lynn, Sutton Bridge, Long Sutton.

We then had a stale ham sandwich, of which we found about half a dozen in the cartridge magazine. We lay down in the punt to get out of the wind and I think I went to sleep. When I next sat up the tide really had begun to flow, but very sluggishly, and it looked like a long wait... We decided that the sea wasn't too bad and it would be best to go back a bit and get into the channel. After all, the longer we waited, the worse would be the sea. We went back, Christopher towing and me sounding... We passed a beacon...

Then an unexpected difficulty came. The bank along which we were towing became a little cliff and, being on a lee shore, we could tow no more… We decided to try to row and got out the oars. The boat had a lot of water in her and we had some difficulty in getting off the lee shore. When at length we did get about three yards out, one wave came the whole length of the punt and took Christopher green, in the back…so whilst he pulled off the shore I feverishly rowed and baled alternately… However, it was some time before I had her empty and by that time the water had become calmer…and soon we were rowing

Christmas trees and coloured lights decorate the appropriately named St Nicholas Street, which winds its way down to the church at Diss

Andrew Dodds

with great relief in comparative comfort... Then at last we came into the straight... We had a mile or more of this and we crossed to the sheltered side of the river. When we had come in sight of the old lighthouses we crossed back again... We pulled into the little 'gull' by the sea-wall then...we climbed up the mud slope and walked along the bank to the lighthouse, immeasurably relieved to be on dry land...

One of the cottagers further along the bank gave us cold milk to drink, and jolly good it was... Then we set off to walk three miles to Sutton Bridge. We got a lift in a car for the last bit. There we hired a car for the remaining ten miles to Lynn.

"We arrived at 11.30," my diary concludes, "having had two stale sandwiches each and a glass of milk since 5.30 a.m. The whole thing turned out very well, but we never deserved to get off so lightly. We undertook a very dangerous thing almost without knowing it until it was too late to turn back, and had any mishap occurred we should have been done - there was no margin of safety. Anyway it gave us both a nasty scare. I never remember to have been so frightened for so prolonged a period. The whole thing was madness, but very good experience and the boat stood up to the seas surprisingly well."

Kazarka was indeed an unqualified success. She was built to the designs of Major Hulse, the Expert, incorporating all the modifications and refinements which he had thought of since his own punt was built. She was probably then the best double punt in the country.

Peter Scott - Abridged from *The Eye of the Wind*. 1961

Today we can follow the Peter Scott Walk for ten miles from the West Lynn ferry to Sir Peter Scott's former home at the lighthouse on the eastern bank of the River Nene near Sutton Bridge. The walk was launched in 1989. It passes through an area that is a haven for wildlife with extensive views across The Wash. Walkers should keep to the sea banks as the tidal marshes are very dangerous.

The ferry does not run on Sundays or on bank holidays.

Henry Williamson (1895-1977) moved from Devon, where he had written *Tarka the Otter*, to farm at Stiffkey shortly before the outbreak of World War II. Although living conditions were still basic, his wife and children joined him there for Christmas:

The Williamson Family's Christmas at Stiffkey

At the station I sent a telegram to Devon, telling the family to come up two or three days before Christmas. We would all live in the granary. If the cottages were not finished by Christmas Eve, they must remain unfinished. The rebuilding had already cost just over £550, to which must be added £200 of the original cost. The woodwork was unpainted, the walls rough with plaster. In some rooms, the original dirty, scaly plaster remained. There were no drains, no cesspit. Bugg Houses had become Williamson's Folly.

I began to feel a rising tremor of excitement within me. The children would now be half-way from London, somewhere beyond Cambridge. They had caught the nine o'clock from Devon, Mother and the five children. The two smallest ones would be tired. I found the inward tremor change to panic. I must hurry: in less than an hour they would be arriving at Whelk station. What should I say to them, expecting to enter a fine new farmhouse home? I had turned the men off; the cottages were made, except for bits of plastering, inside doors, painting, and colouring the walls. But they looked too bare and bleak: the granary was more home-like, draughty and dark as it was.

Putting the tractor in top gear, and with twin gleaming plows in air, I went down fast to the hedge; picked up my dinner bag, slung it over my shoulders, through the new creosoted gate and down the hill, and the half-finished gulley-road, to the cart-shed. Then to the granary, to see the fire glowing in the stove, and blankets and sleeping-bags airing round it... A cup of tea hastily swallowed: I must not be late at the station!... Round to the cart-shed again, push out the old open car...and off along the narrow winding coast road to the station. Ten minutes to wait, time to put the hood up. At last it was puffing round the curve. Would they be there? Supposing something had happened to stop them? Ah, there was one face! Two faces, four faces, five faces, six faces... How are you, Loetitia? I've got some hens, and they actually lay eggs!... I'm afraid the cottages won't be ready just yet, m'dear, but the granary's warm, now I've altered the stove, and the wind's dropped. I've got the hood up, for the small children. Now we're off, we'll soon be there, only four miles. Hark! what's that? A strange jangling, honking, cronkling noise, hundreds of noises all together, high up in the sky. Listen, children! The wild geese coming in from the sea! This is the Coast of the Wild Geese!...

Flocks of the birds were flying inland at intervals all night, we heard them in the granary, as we sat at the long oak table, eating roast pheasant... How the children loved the granary. They ran up and down the stairs, they explored all the dark nooks and caves among the stacked furniture, they thought it ever so much nicer than an ordinary house. While they were undressing overhead, their bare feet running on the boards, I knew then I was right to have brought them here, to the farm... I must not fail them, they were England, the new England. This was only the beginning.

When they all were sleeping upstairs I went outside into the frosty night, and saw the stars again as though for the first time...

In the starlight I climbed the hill, and looked up into the sky, and felt the earth bearing me up, the strong earth, dear earth: and as other men had before me, but wordlessly, I prayed.

Henry Williamson - Abridged from *The Story of a Norfolk Farm.* 1941

Lilias Rider Haggard (1892-1968) was Henry Rider Haggard's youngest daughter. She inherited his literary talent and wrote about her daily life and the Norfolk countryside. Her articles appeared in the *Eastern Daily Press* on Saturdays for many years from 1936 onwards and were collected into *Norfolk Life, Norfolk Notebook* and *A Country Scrap-book.* In *A Country Scrap-book* she describes a wartime Christmas of widespread separation ansd anxiety from her quiet home by the Waveney:

A Wartime Christmas beside the River Waveney

A wild wind roars over the tops of the elms on the crest of the hill, thrashing them back and forth against the sky, but down below in the wood the winter sunshine lies quietly on the bare boles of the trees, and not a twig stirs. It lights up the dark gloss of the ivy, the shining green of the hollies, and turns the crimson berries to little glowing lanterns...

Norfolk at Christmas

It is winter, 'time of little comfort', but we stand at the gate of the year... and who knows what will befall in this England before Christmas comes again? - and after that, when what we have fought for is won? 'Ha! Ha!' says the practical man, rubbing his hands. 'Big business, expanding trade - more ease - more comfort - more money - more cars - that, like the immortal Alice, we may go faster and faster.' An uneasy thought sometimes stirs in the bucolic mind, no doubt dulled by prolonged contemplation of the war-time cabbage.

To where is this wild pursuit of the discoveries of science leading us?

One year later:
From now on, however dark the mornings, our faces are set towards the light. With us autumn has lingered to the very end of December. There are still roses in the garden, frail pale buds, which drop into little pools of faint-scented petals upon the polished table directly you bring them into the warmth of the house. Under the stable wall, and in the long border, hyacinth and crocus are thrusting up fat buds, the

By the beginning of December, the markets leave no doubt as to what is coming. In the Market Place at Aylsham, shoppers and cars mingle with the Christmas trees and market stalls.

Andrew Dodds

daffodils are as forward as the carefully cherished ones in bowls on the window-sill.....

When Nada and I went down to the wood to collect a Christmas tree the hazels were set thick with catkins and the thrushes were singing hard, not the shadowy broken phrases of a month ago, but with the confidence and full promise of April days, a chorus you seldom hear in the east of England before February dawns. There are more of them about than for many months, for three hard winters in succession thinned the thrush population down almost to nothing. Blackbirds, for some reason, stand prolonged frost better, perhaps because of their more wary and vigorous nature.

We chose our Christmas tree carefully; no small seedling thinned out from amongst its crowded fellows, but the slender top of an old tree, whose long straight trunk had already been sawn into props, the graceful branches hung all over with slender cones. Gilded gold and silver with some treasured bottles of paint, the cones will look as lovely as the ornaments no longer procurable.

Every year since I can remember Christmas dinner ended with the same ceremony... The decanters having gone round 'with the sun', my father rose to give the toasts. My mother first, the members of the family who were abroad, always a goodly list, ending up: 'Friends at home and absent - ships at sea - and all round the hat!' As a small child the last phrase used to puzzle me. What, I wondered, could be in that mysterious hat?

A happy Christmas - that heartfelt and loving wish which comes from prison camps, and little ships and battlefields, and sad hearts which spend their time, as one mother wrote to me today, 'sick with anxiety'.

Lilias Rider Haggard - Abridged from *A Country Scrap-book*. 1950

For many people, the Christmas Eve service marks the real start to Christmas. William Rivière captures the wonder of a town-bred teenager with artistic inclinations at finding himself in a Norfolk country church for the first time. The Norfolk landscape and weather are described in vivid word-paintings throughout this book:

Christmas Eve at St. Michael's Church, Barton Turf

Too many people he didn't know. Jolting along bleak lanes through the moonless night, Kit Marsh had arrived aching from being wedged into the back of a shooting-brake with a child that had whined till it was allowed not to go to bed and a terrier that had whined for fifteen miles. Now he stood shivering in his duffle coat, stamping his cold feet on church path gravel.

Mr and Mrs Clabburn he was meant to know, and they were kind. But these Clabburn neighbours, these car-loads of Clabburn cousins he couldn't distinguish from Clabburn brothers and sisters, these Clabburn uncles and aunts, these Clabburn dogs…

Grey figures swathed in coats slammed car doors; sturdy, spectral, they tramped through the gale shuddering in the trees up to the glowing porch. Kit followed. Where was Robert? Not that he knew Robert Clabburn either; he was in his last year at Cambridge and looked dauntingly debonair…but still, Robert was his host…
"Where are we?"
"Where *are* we?"

Robert grinned at the boy shuffling into the pew beside him.

"I mean...I...I can't remember the name of this church."
"Barton Turf. All these muddy villages look the same to you?"
"Oh...Er...In the middle of the night."

Robert knelt down. They were all kneeling down. Kit thudded onto his bony knees, a prayer book fell off an oak ledge. Eyes open, eyes shut? What did one do with one's hands? What did one think if one was these people? If one was him? Already Robert was getting up. Kit sat too.

"Here." Robert shoved a hassock sideways with his foot. "The stone is cold."
"Oh look! What marvellous figures on the screen!"
"It's lovely, isn't it?" Robert murmured, hoping his guest would drop his voice. "Pity some of the faces have been scratched out. Old dissenting country, East Anglia, old Ironside country. When people get up to go to the altar rail, you'll see the paintings better."

The church was packed for Christmas Eve; the congregation took a long time to be given the bread and wine; Kit dwelt on the rood screen panel by panel, passionately committed those defaced figures to his mind, the faded reds and golds on the carved arches. Contented now, he resolved he would never again be unnerved by rigmarole and piety. That was awful, he must outgrow it. What would his mother think? She would smile. Thinking of her made him smile, sitting at midnight in the nave made gorgeous by candles, by holly and ivy, the solitary figure in the pew, a rank of Clabburns kneeling in the chancel. London and his mother seemed a long way off, his mother whose name was no longer Mrs Marsh (there was a Mrs Marsh, but Kit's father had married her in Muscat, they never visited England), his mother who though she never suggested going to church took him most weeks to a concert or a play...

As the service ended, he had wanted to ask Robert if he believed in God or did he come to church because it was a likeable social occasion and to accompany his parents? Trailing out down the aisle, he had wanted to tell the choir how much he had enjoyed their singing, but it never occurred to him he might have the courage to accost one of those surpliced figures chatting gaily by the font. Then the parson had shaken his hand and he had felt embarrassed that the cleric's manner repelled him. And now Robert said they were going to a party.

"Come on, Kit, you can't have forgotten. We're going to Fen House, to the Dobells. Just for a drink. They're old friends, you'll like them."

Who was that girl hurrying away down the path into the night, fair hair whipping out from her hat? Had she been in church and he never noticed?

William Rivière - Abridged from *Watercolour Sky*. 1990

The names of Sylvia Townsend Warner (1893-1978) and Valentine Ackland are linked with Sloley, Winterton and Salthouse as well as the county of Dorset. They spent the winter of 1950-51 living at Great Eye Folly, a former coastguard station on the shingle ridge at Salthouse, with no modern conveniences whatsoever, accompanied by Niou, their Siamese cat. It was a winter of post-war austerity made worse by the Korean War

Sylvia Townsend Warner's published diary and letters reveal her undiminished enthusiasm for life in this beautiful but desolate spot a few yards from the breaking waves. It was to be a very severe winter:

Winter at Great Eye Folly, Salthouse

October 1950
27. Still cold - and still tired we drove to G.E.F. [Great Eye Folly]
The fire was lit downstairs, there was tea ready for us... Dreamily
we read, unpacked, listened to the sea: it was the view from the upper
room that suddenly woke us to a sense of place, and we knew we
were here. We unpacked, put away, put out - it was almost dusk
before we went out again, and picked up our first driftwood.

28. ...An intensely stormy day - we saw the sea darken and grow
sullen, and an hour later it was rent with white horses. ...we went off
to the local stores, and bought staples like potatoes and toilet-paper,
and then on to Holt, over a russet heath and through a violent
hailstorm. Valentine bought nails at a shop resounding with
anecdotes of cats, and everyone had Norfolk manners, and we much
approve of Holt...

November
2. ...In the morning of this fine calm day Niou was out playing
among the fortifications - so stilly couched that we thought him a sea-
white stone. Then I walked to the post, and heard about the flood of
/47 and how a wave broke the shop-window and swept the wool off
its shoulder-high shelf.

14. ...Still cold, windy, with brilliant colours on the marsh. Its dykes
are now full of ruffled water - the curious look of the inland waterway
flowing under the steep bank of sea-pebbles on our eastern beach. I
darned a sheet - Niou killed two rats - and we drove in the afternoon
round and about the Holt Heath.

20. ...I walked alone, by the sea's edge till I felt, like an animal - this is beyond any breathed air; and so it was, for climbing onto the shingle bank I found myself among the marrom tufts, and seeing a superb piece of marsh: the pale sharp poppy-horns standing above green frizzed cushions, marsh michaelmas daisy in thick grey thistledown mackerel-sky clouds, and the marsh water like blue lead above cushions of green moss and edged with rust-dark vegetation. I got a quantity of wood too, looking east to Salthouse church under a dark purple cloud.

25. We have now most exquisite moonlight nights with foam as white as goatsmilk or Niou's bosom...

December
15. Snow, hard frost, blizzards, icy roads... So we filled pails and buckets with snow, that sat in front of fires like large wet geese, refusing to thaw... In the afternoon a terrific blizzard: the wind round to the north, and at gale force ever since, so in addition to hoarding water we may be flooded. But a most happy day, for all that.

16. ...the landscape still mostly snow, and the wind icy: it blows to us from Yorkshire & Lincolnshire, which are deep in snow...

Christmas gifts and mail were delivered by the post-girl battling across the marsh against strong winds. A new translation of the *Letters of Marcel Proust* from her publisher at Chatto and Windus gave Sylvia Townsend Warner great pleasure and its illustrations brought back memories of youthful visits to France. There was a Bechstein piano at Eye Folly, so this would have been a Christmas, their only Christmas in this wild place, filled with music and books and happiness.

January 1951

10. ...A conversation with Mrs Gray - she still had no candles and no matches. They had been told there would be no [gas] cartridges for the next 3 months [...] On the same day, she had been told that price of knitting wool would go up from 1/8 oz to 2/8; and Mr Gray had learned at the garage that there would be very few small spare parts, as the factories were working - if at all - a 36 hour week because of the call-up of metal. She referred blastingly to the Festival of Britain (Oh! I forgot - they can expect very few tinned foods, no tin)...

King's Lynn Shopping Centre 1971.

Eastern Daily Press

23. ...We set out for Brancaster, but in Wells on Sea the gears had a fit of impotence. [...] In Holt we learned with sorrow that taking down the gear-box, etc, would be a matter of 4 days - even if renewal parts could be got. Vauxhall Motors has now gone over entirely to armament vehicles...

February
2. A frittering day - and one of the coldest I have ever known. A south wind, again: a steady stealthy boring wind; and no sign of it, on this clean-shaved landscape, except on the sea. As the waves - very small ones, approached the shore, the wind turned them backward, aborted them: instead of breaking, they faded out on the sea, one following another, like bars on a mackerel...

4. Sunday. And a tearing gale...

11. ...This morning there was a violent n.e. gale...and indoors, the kitchen a swamp, the larder a waterfall, and fountains of wind blown sink-water blowing up from the runaway... But in flashes through the windows I saw how wildly lovely it was - and in the afternoon, the wind going down and the rain ceasing, I walked along the beach admiring the sea...

21. ...Mrs Gray has given up being a grocer, because there are so few groceries, so much paper work, and the margin of profit has been cut again...

March
20. We left [Great Eye Folly] at 8.30...

1953
February
1. On the 6 p.m. news, the news of the flood on the east coast - all Holderness under salt water, Yarmouth & Lynn inundated, and the seaward end of Sea Palling flooded, with people drowned...

2. An aerial photograph in the Daily Mail seems to be Salthouse, though it was called Sheringham. Either way, ruin and desolation, with a great elbow of sea thrust inland...

3. A letter...today tells of all the coast road houses in ruins or so badly damaged as to be uninhabitable... The sea came in, not by the Folly Gap, but sweeping from Cley, and swept through the Dun Cow, and the Post-Office...

6. ...In the afternoon, the postman came up the drive with a letter... The seaward wall of G.E.F. has fallen, the house stands open to the sea...

Sylvia Townsend Warner - Abridged from *The Diaries of Sylvia Townsend Warner* edited by Claire Harman. 1994

Sylvia Townsend Warner had already written *The Corner that Held Them,* published in 1954, about a fictional Benedictine nunnery at Oby, and was writing *The Flint Anchor*, a family story of obsession and inflexible rectitude, set in a fictional town called Loseby on the north Norfolk coast.

When Lilias Rider Haggard declared to the editor of the *Eastern Daily Press* that she was "written out" in 1949 a new country writer was needed. Eric Fowler suggested the name of Adrian Bell and borrowed the agricultural editor's car to drive to Redisham in Suffolk to speak to the author of *Corduroy. A Countryman's Notebook* was born: it delighted Saturday readers for thirty years, the remainder of Adrian Bell's life:

A Countryman's Christmas Notebooks: 1953-1977

17 January 1953 - *The Dancers*
It occurred to me, as I laid aside my rarely assumed dinner jacket, that we do not dance enough...

The label on my dinner jacket reminded me it was made in Bury St. Edmunds 25 years ago. This dress suit meant much to me then. In a farmhouse ten miles from anywhere it became a symbol. In no other walk of life are the clothes of the day and the clothes of the night more in contrast. Hedging and dancing usually went together, or muck-carting and dancing. They shared the same season...

4 January 1958 - *The Spiral Stair*
December 17th 1957 - Breaking up ceremony at village school... I joined in singing *Little Town of Bethlehem*, a suitable choice, with fields all around, since its tune is an old folk song, *"The Ploughboy's Dream."*... A carol service at the Grammar School the same evening. Some intricate part singing, beautifully modulated and controlled. My only duty was to read a lesson...

24th - Some fine holiday fish already being caught - in retrospect, across the inn table...

25th - After the Queen's speech, rowed up-river, alone among birds and regiments of golden reeds. Afternoon sky full of blushful clouds with blue flecks and daffodil spaces. Two swans followed my boat home.

Then, for those few days between Christmas and the New Year, we had a sense, as at no other time, of time almost standing still. Festivity was for the moment exhausted... Hiatus - occupied with finishing Christmas viands alone, selfishly, with grunt of satisfaction and gnawing of bone, and holding up of bottle to the light...

And then, the bells carolled that we have started the merry-go-round all over again...

19 December 1959 - *Creative Leisure*

I see an abundance of toys, and they have a large audience, a grown-up audience in intense inward debate; "Is he old enough for that?" "Might a baby swallow that, or any part of it?" "Are the eyes firmly fixed?" Is there any toy that cannot, on occasion, be used as an offensive weapon or an instrument of *felo de se*?

Looking at these toyshops stocked, even stuffed, with toys. I wondered were we lucky? We didn't think so at the time; we were at our wits' end to know what to fill our children's stockings with, what to hang on the tree for them. Because it was war time; toyshops were empty and closed... People came to our aid. A huge teddy bear, grown-out-of, was offered, with patched elbows and in need of re-whiskering. But he was received with joy and loved.

2 January 1960 - *Frost on my Tea*

December is over. It seems much more than three weeks since the first Christmas card arrived...a picture of a unit of sub-standard rural housing (at least that is what our sanitary officer would call it) in a cold snap... Next day my cousin Mabel's card arrived from Maryland. It was, as usual, one of those lovely Christmas cards that work. Last year when you opened it a flight of robins took off from a tree. This year Santa Claus drained a glass of ale, which miraculously replenished itself when you closed the card. All the family took turns with that card, until the sand (which was the beer) began to leak out.

The cards are still our picture gallery, but the holiday is over...
Delightful interval, when the family, home for Christmas, insisted on
doing the fires for me, and raker noises reverberating up through the
chimney became church bells in a dream.

13 January 1962 - *A Time of Licence*
I slithered to the Post Office to find queues gathered there.
Sometimes I wonder if a limit is ever going to be put to the functions
that are delegated to the Post Office...

Now the P.O. is both tax collector and almoner, bank, stationer and
citizens' advice bureau...

December 1960 Norwich Civic Carol Concert on the steps of City Hall
Eastern Daily Press

In addition to all this, it becomes during the first fortnight of the year a motor licence office. It was seeing the queue at the counter which reminded me of my own. I went straight home and began the annual hunt for the registration book, which I make a rule of keeping in One Safe Place, and twelve months is the utmost limit of my being able to guess with any probability which that one safe place may be. I comfort myself, "Well, I've never lost it yet." Sure enough, I found it in the place where I first looked, at the third time of looking there.

Several things are then needed. First a skewer with which to dislodge the circle of spring wire which keeps the back of the licence-holder in place. This wire pings away into the darkness. Next a torch is required to find where it has pinged to. Then to find the insurance certificate, and make sure (where are my spectacles?) that it is not the road-worthiness certificate.

At last, having filled in the form and made out the cheque, I bundled all these documents into my over-coat pocket and went and dumped them on the counter of the Post Office. But the old licence disc was no longer there. Vanishing trick. On such occasions I feel I ought to have been a conjuror: things vanish without me even trying to make them. I found it had hidden itself in a price list of Lacon's Christmas Ales.

So that is over for another twelve months; one of the small but cumulative fusses from which the early Christian fathers were exempt, as also are Eskimos and, until recently, the islanders of Tristan da Cunha...

20 January 1962 - *Back to Normal*
On Christmas Day, I put up a kingfisher, a heron, several snipe and peewits all within fifty yards, as I walked on the marshes. And met here and there a solitary, non-Christmassy-looking person; a man in new gloves to whom in all that marsh loneliness I said "Good afternoon," it being Christmas Day. He seemed rather surprised at

the greeting and responded perfunctorily. One might have thought he was an anti-Christmas person, such as you occasionally find in the novels of Dickens, but for the new gloves...

After breakfast my wife produced gloves for the family and an umbrella for me, wrapped in multi-coloured "Merry Christmas" paper, which I for a moment thought hopefully might be the colour of the umbrella.

22 December 1962 - *Bringing Home the Tree*
My wife came home and said she had bought a Christmas tree. She added, in extenuation, that it was only a very little Christmas tree. I think she has been secretly wanting to start having a Christmas tree again for a long time - ever since we gave it up when our family had reached ages of 17-plus, and drank to one another sedately across the turkey, and didn't any longer pull crackers, or wear fancy hats...

Festive sparkle at Womack Water. A scene from Edward Seago's garden.

Photograph by *Mrs Peter Seymour*

One of the pleasures of having a family was that you started Christmas trees again. And when you start a grand-family, you can start having Christmas trees yet once more. I said to my wife: "But our grandson Richard is only eighteen months old; he won't understand about a Christmas tree." She replied: "His mother was only one year old when we had our first one on the table." I recalled her large and wondering eyes at the lighted candles and the tinsel, her spoon suspended and dinner temporarily forgotten. That Christmas tree, one foot high, lasted us right through the years, from one to 17. Of course, the tree received a check every time it was lifted and had its roots crammed into a bucket, and endured a fortnight of ordeal by candlegrease in a hot room. Even so, that 18-year-old tree did take some shifting that last time, and was dragged through the hall with difficulty, setting all the pictures swinging. It reached the ceiling, and had to be decorated from a step-ladder... After that - well, it's a sad story. We moved house, and could not bring the tree with us; there was so much else to bring. I paid a return visit to the old home the following March. Imagine my feelings when I found a sawn-off stump where the tree had stood. The new owners of the house had simply amputated the tree and stuck it in a tub. It lay sere and dead in a corner by the rubbish heap.

My wife said, "If you are passing that way, you might fetch our new Christmas tree home..."

When I got the tree home, I put it in a pail filled with compost to keep it in good heart; and there it sits, buried in a garden bed, awaiting the day... We still have the candle-holders from long ago, and the old silvered glass balls. I was surprised that my wife knew just where to put her hand on these. She must have been long looking forward to a Christmas tree again...

10 December 1966 - *Two Cheers for Winter*
I have just received a gift of the *"E.D.P."* Calendar for 1967. God send that the lovely scenes pictured therein will be with us through

1967, and no enormous new barrack town, marina, casino, or other annihilator of green shades and pure waters be dumped on, say, Shelfanger ("Peaceful Afternoon") or Santon Downham ("Filtering Sunlight").

Here are East Anglian lanes which hardly contradict what are for me the most poignant features of *"A Country Camera: 1844-1914,"* which another friend has given me...

So I turn the leaves of these twin pleasures of a winter evening, a little surprised at how many photographs from 1900 onwards I can recall as being part of my everyday experience as a child.

30 December 1967 - *Rest us Merry*
It was raining in Bethlehem too. Saw son standing under a mackintosh in a deserted town square. Christmas Eve in Bethlehem... Suddenly, as nothing else could do, rain in Bethlehem brought the Christmas story home to us...

17 January 1970 - *A Long Quiet Time*
City guests are intrigued to see us still fiddling with sticks and matches, feeding real flames with real fuel... We would not be without our stoves, and the logs that lie therein licking themselves with small quick tongues of flame, as cats lick their fur...

1 January 1972 - *It Comes Round Again*
...To defend the mind and sharpen the senses is my recipe for happiness in 1972...

15 December - 1973 *That Little Candle*
When I read that Norwich was abandoning its open-air carol service and civic Christmas tree, I rather hoped there would be protests in the correspondence column...

Traditionally, in my time-scale, Christmas carols were sung under the stars. We survivors of the "lamp room" age can recall many glimmering carol services in untrafficked little market-town squares, sometimes under a full moon...

I even think the energy crisis is a blessing not in disguise when I remember how in the war we lit our tree with saved candle-ends, and the children gazed and were happy...

St. Nicholas', Blakeney

Painting by *Derek Essex*

31 December 1977 - *Reduce Speed Now*
Hey Presto, another Saturday, and it all begins again. New Year Sunday, hogmanay, handfast, first foot, holiday Monday, absentee Tuesday... And why not?

As we all begin to go round the immemorial circuit of the new year, isn't it time to think a new thought? Of all that is written in the Press, or talked on the box, has anybody asked, let alone answered, why is it taken as holy writ that unless more things are made and sold ... we are falling off? And why is advertising our god?

I read this morning that the country's prospects are rosy, only that production lags. We are using up the earth's once-for-all mineral wealth at a reckless rate as it is, so why should it be virtuous to boast of producing yet more and raiding posterity's nest-egg of mineral resources?

Adrian Bell - Abridged from *A Countryman's Notebooks. Eastern Daily Press*

Eric Fowler wrote under the pseudonym Jonathan Mardle. His book *Wednesday Mornings* contained a collection of his essays including *The Magic of Lights* which had a Christmas theme and appeared in the *Eastern Daily Press* on December 14th 1949. My Christmastime favourite is *Going to the Fair*. It first appeared in 1961 and is included in *The Best of Jonathan Mardle*. He describes waking as a child on Christmas morning to the sound of the bells of St. Peter Mancroft and the delights of the Christmas Fair held on the Old Cattle Market below Norwich Castle.

Edward Seago (1910-1974) the famous landscape painter was born in Norwich. His autobiography, *A Canvas to Cover,* appeared in 1947, and a biography, *Edward Seago: The Other Side of the Canvas,* by Jean Goodman, was published in 1978.

After travelling widely, Edward Seago settled in the village of Ludham. He bought Walnut House, a Dutch-style house with mellow, red brick walls, leaded windows and a gabled roof, and renamed it the Dutch House. The house had been built in 1603.

Peter Cushing, the actor, one of Edward Seago's friends, was invited to stay at the Dutch House at Christmas. Field Marshall Sir Claude Auchinleck was also a guest:

"It was a house that lent itself to Christmas": Edward Seago and the Dutch House, Ludham

Long before Cushing met Seago he had been an admirer of the painter's work and after one of the early post-war exhibitions wrote to tell him so. In reply came a pleasant, formal acknowledgement from Ludham. Four years later Cushing and his wife were visiting friends in Cromer where, on an impulse, the actor telephoned Seago to say he was in the neighbourhood and asked if he could call and see some more paintings. Seago explained that he was leaving for Portugal the following day so the visit would have to be that same evening. The Cushings came, the friendship was immediate, and it was five o'clock the next morning before the visitors left Seago's house. It was agreed that they would be back there to spend Christmas.

'It was a house that lent itself to Christmas,' Cushing said, recalling some fifteen Christmases he and his wife Helen spent there. 'It was decorated with holly and candles and a Christmas tree and there were presents and games round the fire and - always - laughter. We were usually the only house-guests but Auchinleck and his sister often joined us in the evening for Christmas dinner and Ted's parents and

John were there. I remember one game we played which was a sort of charade called "How to Cheat the Customs Man" and the Field-Marshal excelled at this.'

At one time, some of the laughter was engendered by plays Seago wrote for his friends to act out with him on his tape-recorder. For many years it was his favourite toy and at Christmas he prepared the script for a play in which Cushing voiced all the female parts, Seago took the lead and there were supporting roles for everyone...

Jean Goodman - Abridged from *Edward Seago: The Other Side of the Canvas*. 1990

Since leaving Cambridge University in 1965, David Chaffe has worked for the conservation of British native wildlife and the wild places where it lives and thrives. He spent time working at the Otter Trust at Earsham, near Bungay, and now has an otter sanctuary at Weare Giffard close to the River Torridge, in the area where Henry Williamson's story *Tarka the Otter* was set.

David Chaffe's first otter cub was born in Norfolk:

Tiki - The Wanderer

It had been Boxing Day 1966 when Bob Cooke, a man of the marshes, rang me from his remote cottage on the north Norfolk coast. I had met both him and his wife Joan a few years earlier and prior to my three years at university; he bred wildfowl as a hobby and I had acquired many young birds from him for my own collection. But that day, in late December, his message was that whilst checking the coastline, for he was also an auxiliary coastguard, he had spotted a very wet half-grown otter cub stranded in a tidal creek on Salthouse marsh. His English springer spaniel had successfully 'fetched', so could I come and collect it straightaway.

Otter cubs are born blind and helpless with soft grey velvety fur and weigh seventy-eight grams. They have rather square muzzles, tiny ears, small pads and are blessed with half-webbed feet, all of which are pink in colour. They suckle every two or three hours, pressing the bitch's stomach with their front paws; their little tails wag and as their mother moves to re-settle, the cubs will call softly.

Their development is slow; their eyes open when they are about five weeks old and weaning begins at seven weeks. From about ten weeks they will eat solid food more regularly. But they will continue to be nursed for up to six months and will not finally split from their mother until a year after they are born...

That journey, returning with a half-grown otter cub, was dramatic enough to have remained deeply etched on my mind ever since.

That phone call had come when, with my family, we were concluding Boxing Day lunch. I had come down from Cambridge eighteen months previously and was in the process of creating my Wildlife Park in Westbury-on-Trym, Bristol; the Park was to be opened to the general public six months hence in June 1967 by my then schoolboy hero, Peter Scott.

I had made many friends in Norfolk from those Cambridge days where I had planned my future life and work. My first fallow deer fawns had come from the Earl of Leicester's estate at Holkham Hall; they had then been bottle-reared, and now formed the nucleus of a splendid little herd...

Bob had briefly reported that he had been walking the nearby saltmarsh and the adjacent coastal shingle ridge close to his home. This he did regularly at first light every day, at the same time exercising his dog. For no particular reason that morning, and as luck would have it, he took a different route. Much later he had decided to return skirting a marsh that was split by a main freshwater drainage ditch, and via a track which gave him, at the same time, a close view of the top end of the tidal creek. Just as he was turning for home he had spotted it, a half-grown otter cub, apparently exhausted and soaking wet, lying amongst the debris that is found at the top of the tide. It was so distressed that his dog had retrieved it without fuss, although the springer had needed all its expertise to cope with the soft mud. Bob had experienced no difficulty in tucking it inside his duffel coat next to his heavy duty all weather clothing. On his return, he had immediately wrapped it in a couple of old sweaters and had placed it on a bed of towels in a cardboard box. Safe next to the all-night stove, his instincts told him it might now stand a chance of surviving in that warmth, but there would have been none at all if it had been left exposed to the winter's elements out on the marsh. The weather was bitterly cold and as he returned to his cottage close to the coast road, further heavy rain had started.

"Can you come and collect it as soon as possible?" he had enquired.
"Yes, of course," I replied instantly, and almost before his question was finished.
"The sooner it's being properly cared for the better," he had continued. "When do you think you could come? Joan and I will obviously do our best in the meantime."
"I can come straightaway, now, this afternoon," I interrupted again.
"That would be best; the sooner it's safe in a new and stable environment with you, the sooner it might recover from its setback. You're very welcome to stay overnight."
"I'll be on my way as soon as I am organised and I'll try and be with you by late tonight. I'll ring if there are any problems," I added excitedly as I returned to the dining table.

A few minutes later the implications of his unexpected call were sinking in; a possible otter cub as the latest arrival for my Park, and in the middle of winter too... Everybody joined in helping me prepare for an imminent departure; my mother put up some food for the journey and my father made numerous phone calls to discover the whereabouts of the nearest petrol station that might be open on this Bank Holiday. Both the tank and a spare can for the long journey needed to be filled. It was a journey which without hold-ups would take the rest of that day and evening. The final miles would be through the lonely and deserted lanes of rural north Norfolk, not a trip to be normally undertaken in poor weather, ever alone in the height of winter.

Bob's phone call...had been very brief, with no more than the bare details. It was important to think and plan rationally. I would surely need a travelling crate; what and when was I going to try and feed the cub; was it still on its mother's milk or would it eat solid food, fish perhaps? A suitable box was eventually found, as were some straw bales to pack around it as extra insulation; I eased out a couple of frozen mackerel and herring from much larger packs, fish that I already had in store for my seals. I asked my father to find a chemist or to check with a local hospital early the following morning after the Bank Holiday break, in order to obtain some dried milk and a bottle feeder ready for my return. The cub could well have been younger than Bob at first thought.

Suddenly there was no more time to plan. It was already early afternoon and I needed to be on my way... Admittedly it was a route I already knew from going backwards and forwards to University. From Cambridge and Newmarket and beyond, heading further east was another already familiar stretch too...

I have no real recollection over thirty years later of most of that journey across central England, except that the weather seemed to be worsening, was becoming steadily colder and wetter, and that the already poor daylight of that Boxing Day afternoon had soon vanished. What does stay quite dramatically in my mind, though, was the final few miles through the lanes from Holt along the valley of the River Glaven, before meeting the coastal road running from Blakeney through to Cley-next-the-Sea. Bob and Joan's cottage would be eventually found at the far end of the magnificent blanket of coastal marsh and reclaimed fields that lie behind the shingle ridge at Salthouse...

By now it was very late, gone eleven o'clock, and with over two hundred and fifty miles already on the clock, I used my previous knowledge of those lanes to avoid going through the small market town of Holt. Some five years before, in the spring of 1961, I had left Clifton College to work with the naturalist Philip Wayre for two summers at his Norfolk home... I had originally become aware of those north Norfolk marshes while still at school, and with my parents had enjoyed a summer caravan holiday close to Blakeney. I spent hours seeking out the bearded tits in the reedbeds of Cley marsh...

Holt, and more particularly the Feathers Inn, had become for me the place to socialise out of term time with new friends of similar interests. However, in the pitch black of this wild winter's night, I sensed that most sensible souls would have been indoors, closeted around a roaring winter fire.

There was no doubt in my mind that the wind had now strengthened to a severe gale; there were frequent squally gusts which served to focus my mind on the fact that, at long last, I was coming close to my goal...

I recalled how Bob had previously recounted to me tales of the otters that frequent the water meadows and fresh-water drains of the empty north Norfolk marshes with their endless reedbeds and tidal creeks. These stretch for miles from Scolt Head Island to the west to the last of the drainage ditches which divide the meadows used for the summer grazing in the east. Bob and his wife Joan lived in a two storey cottage that looked out over this wildlife haven towards the vast shingle ridge that protected them and the other homes that hugged the coast road, from the worst of the ravages of the North Sea storms...

In winter the farm stock and the summer bird-watchers deserted the marshes, and the solitude was only occasionally shattered by a weekend wildfowler. On that night the nearest rutted and waterlogged fields to the road, and the ditches which were lying almost brimful, were home to a host of wigeon and teal, and to many sheltering waders and winter migrants... Windswept, desolate and very cold, I was surprised the marshes were so well favoured by all and sundry, unless of course you had climbed the protective shingle ridge and had suffered the full blast of the arctic wind as it whipped in off the North Sea.

You could lean at almost forty-five degrees forward into the gale...

I remembered suddenly braking hard to turn right to join the main coastal road from Blakeney. There was no oncoming traffic that late at night, and I was down the short hill to cross the river Glaven where the sluice gates keep the ebb and flow of the tidal waters of the marshes apart from the fresh water streams of the meadows... Next it was sharp left, and through Cley past the windmill and church, with welcoming lights still lit late in a few homes. As I broke cover from the village I passed the last cottages on the higher ground on my right and with the marshes coming up on my left, I suddenly felt the storm with dramatic effect.

The van lurched as the ferocity and the force of the threatening gale was thrown against the side of the vehicle. I put the windscreen wipers in overdrive as the squally rain turned to sleet. The late night temperature had dropped fast. Rain, wind and sleet, everything seemed to be coming from over my left shoulder, lashing against the passenger window of the van as I tried to hurry the last couple of miles to my destination. My heart was beating faster now for my expectations had been building rapidly since passing Holt a few miles back. The excitement had dried my mouth. Even in the darkness I recognised the village duck pond of Salthouse but further away, marshside, I could not make anything out clearly. There was nothing but the sound of wind and rain.

Then it was a right-hand indicator before the final braking and suddenly I was, at long last, swinging up into the welcoming shelter of the courtyard alongside Bob's cottage. I was late, very late, but I had made it. It was almost midnight.

I grabbed my overnight bag, locked the van and ran into the lower porch to escape the elements.

"Come ya in David," Joan called out from the top of the stairs, "you've been a long while, we'd given you up for lost. It's a terrible night out there. You'll have a cup of tea, something to eat?"

The living-room was a snug fortress against the wild elements that the North Sea throws against the east coast, and as I stepped into its warm glow there was Bob, relaxed as always, in his favourite armchair. His face broke into a slight smile, and with a twinkle in his eyes both of mischief and affection he greeted me.

"How ya doing then?," he enquired in his soft Norfolk accent.
"Fine," I replied, "just fine, although very cold. But I'll warm up in here in no time."

The living room was at first floor level, simply because there is always the continual threat of a tidal surge in the North Sea breaking the sea defences, as it had done on a dreadful winter's night some fifteen years previously. Then there had been a terrible loss of life, property and livestock. On the outside wall of the cottage is a marker at an unbelievable height, indicating the level the waters reached after breaking through the shingle ridge. It was frightening to imagine that at the peak of that storm and at the full tidal surge, there was nothing but the sea for mile upon mile, lying to a depth of several feet...

"I can do you eggs and bacon," called Joan from by the stove, "in the meantime here's your tea. Get that down you straight away, I should think you need it. Then have another with your meal."

"Have you ever seen an otter cub before?" interrupted Bob.
"No, never," I said, "I was hoping perhaps....."
"Of course you can, she's wrapped up in some of my old sweaters. It's a bitch cub by the way, and she's in a box close to the all-night boiler. When I picked her up after the dog had fetched her, she was wet through and cold, but I quickly wrapped her inside my jacket and hurried home. She's been hidden under my clothes since and has dried off remarkably well. Her breathing is now quite regular and she's much bigger than I originally thought. I guess she's ten or maybe even twelve weeks of age."

Although Bob continued to recall the details of the events that had led to her recovery earlier in the day, I...found myself quite simply staring at this beautiful little creature. From above, she appeared to be a deep chocolate brown colour, but as I observed her more closely, and as she occasionally changed her position, I began to appreciate the more delicate shades of lighter brown and grey of her underbody hair and of her inner coat.

"I reckon she's a brave little bitch but by following her mother was rather too bold for her own good," Bob continued. "The holts and the couches where the bitch is lying up with the cubs, and there are sure to be several, must be way out on the marsh. Although the cub could probably swim, she either could not keep up with the bitch, or mother and cub simply became separated by a strong ebbing tide in the main channel. When the tide turns here you know, the waters quickly drain away. I've rarely seen a cub on the outer marshes at this age; it probably tired quickly, became

increasingly waterlogged and found herself stranded away from cover…
She was lucky I found her when I did and that my dog could reach her
across the soft mud."

I was not really listening to Bob. Here at my feet was a most lovely and
delicate creature. She was fast asleep, curled up ever so tightly like so
many family pussycats, in the position which in later years I was to come
to know so well.

"I still can't believe it," I repeated… "Have you fed her?" However
before Bob could respond Joan was interrupting.

"Are you going to come and eat your food? Little-un will be best off
asleep 'til morning."

It was one of the most enjoyable and satisfying suppers I've ever enjoyed,
especially at that hour in the morning.

Not long later I was fading fast in my sleeping bag. An otter cub was
something totally new to me and was instantly most captivating. As I
rapidly lost consciousness I had no idea whatsoever how much the skill of
Bob's springer way out on Salthouse marsh earlier that Boxing Day, was
to influence my future.

David Chaffe - Abridged from *Stormforce*. 1999

Mary Mackie has written a series of books to take the general public,
in imagination at least, behind the scenes in the great houses of the
National Trust to see life, and the fee-paying public, from the other
side of the red rope barrier.

Her years at Felbrigg Hall involved her in a mixture of hard work,
satisfaction, drama and laughter:

All part of the service:
Behind the scenes in a National Trust restaurant

One gloomy Sunday during my stint as tearoom manager, trouble brewed off-stage. It was one of those 'dark days before Christmas' when the dawn seems too weary to push aside the last vestiges of night and all day the world is wrapped in cloudy gloaming, only too willing to give way to a new night's first beckoning finger. Not many people came Christmas shopping on that day, and Lilian and I, in the tearoom, wondered if we were ever going to get rid of the big urn of soup we had made

Over in the Park Restaurant the tale was different. Joan and her staff were bustling about serving a full house. Her special Christmas lunches, served on every Sunday in December, are always fully booked well in advance and that day was no exception. The early starters were well into their main course and the later people were beginning to arrive when, to Joan's horror, an extra party of six turned up. They were not down on the list, but the gentleman in charge of the party insisted he had booked a table, in the name of Smith.

'I phoned and made the reservation myself only yesterday,' he informed the embarrassed Joan in tones which threatened to reach the ears of other diners.

Such a mistake in our system seemed unlikely, but no one is infallible. 'I don't understand what can have happened,' Joan said. 'We've been fully booked for ages. I'm terribly sorry. Who did you speak to?'

'I didn't ask his name! I booked a table for six. For today, at one o'clock. He said that would be in order.'

'It was a man?'

'Certainly it was a man.' Mr Smith was not best pleased. He could see that the tables were rapidly filling as other parties who *were* on the list arrived and took their places. 'And he definitely promised us there would be a table available. What are you going to do about it?'

'If you wouldn't mind waiting a minute...' Joan hurried off to phone Chris and explain the situation. Had *he* taken the booking?

He had not - he had turned down several hopefuls because he knew the tables had all been booked for some time. The only other possibility was Eddie.

Joan told Chris that she would ask Mr Smith and his friends if they would mind waiting a while in the hope that a table might clear before too long, though from previous experience she knew that was unlikely. When people settle down to a Christmas lunch at Felbrigg they like to take their time and it is often four o'clock or after before they finally depart, which is why the entire restaurant is reserved solely for these special meals on December Sundays.

Chris went off to find Eddie, who was cleaning the glass lanterns in the Bird Corridor. His answer was just what Chris had expected: knowing that the restaurant was full, he had not taken any extra bookings, and certainly not yesterday. Since he and Chris were the only men around to answer the phone, the mystery remained.

While they were talking, Joan came over from the main restaurant in the stableyard to say that Mr Smith was becoming restive and ever more angry. Would Chris please come and speak to him?

Chris would. He was always available as a last resort to deal with tricky situations, wherever and whenever they might arise. It is his contention that anyone can make a mistake; how they deal with the consequences is what matters. In this case, since the mistake appeared to be ours - however mystifyingly - he and Joan agreed that the only thing to do would be to offer Mr Smith and party a free lunch, if they wouldn't mind taking it in the Old Kitchen.

On their way back to the stables and the Park Restaurant, they stopped off to warn Lilian and me of what was happening. We were to be ready with glasses of sherry as a first offering to smooth ruffled feathers.

Faced with the by-now fuming Mr Smith, Chris could only apologize for what must have been a break-down in our booking routine. Perhaps the party would care to lunch in the Old Kitchen…at Felbrigg's expense, of course. It was quieter there, anyway, the ambience perhaps even more conducive to a celebratory lunch, with rows of gleaming copper pans on the walls and the ghosts of many other Christmases swirling in the air.

'Well…' Mr Smith allowed himself to be somewhat mollified. 'As it happens I do prefer the Old Kitchen. So much more cosy. Very well. You did say a *free* lunch…?'

So they trooped over to the Old Kitchen, through the newly renovated stable and the lobby of the new toilet block, down an alley between buildings, and across the spacious grass courtyard to the green door, all in the gloom of a dark December day. Lilian and I greeted them with smiles and complimentary sherry, showing them to the table we had hurriedly prepared in festive array. Fortunately, other visitors were still few, so Mr Smith and his party had the Old Kitchen tearoom almost to themselves, under that huge high ceiling where, of old, cooks and potboys had toiled amid steam and roasting fires.

While all preserved an outward show of insouciance, behind the scenes there was chaos and puzzlement. Joan returned to her duties in the Park, where her staff were busy looking after their full house. The rest of us switched gear to cope with Mr Smith.

In the tearoom we didn't have the proper plates and dishes, or the food promised on the special Christmas menu. Everything had to be brought over from the Park Restaurant. While Lilian and I switched on warming ovens and cleared spaces, and looked after both the Smith party and other customers who came in for snacks, Chris rushed to and fro, first bringing a great pan of soup, with dishes in which to serve it.

Christmas at North Lynn Over 60s party 1971

Eastern Daily Press

This journeying between Park Restaurant and Old Kitchen was a bit like doing several circuits of the Grand National course. The new restaurant kitchens are at the far end of the stable block, and the restaurant windows overlook the stable-yard; anyone coming to or going from the kitchen by the quickest route from the Hall would, on that day, be in full view of dozens of merry lunchers. By now they were well into their meal and their wine, wearing paper hats and pulling crackers, the noise of laughter and conversation spilling out with the electric light to enliven the afternoon dusk. Chris didn't want to raise speculation by appearing, like a manic spectre at the feast, rushing backward and forward across the stableyard with trays of comestibles. He went by the back way, his route lying through tenants' gardens, round shrubs and hedges, between bushes, and over flowerbeds and little fences, via wicket gates and narrow stone steps to a final latched gateway under an arch and into the grass courtyard. Branches caught at his clothes and hair, the steps were slippery with damp and lichen, the trays were shiny, the plates kept sliding...

While Lilian and I served the soup, Chris made several journeys to bring plates of turkey, chipolatas, roast and purée potatoes, Brussels sprouts, *petits pois*, stuffings, sauces, and gravy. All went into the warming ovens along with the big dinner plates which he also brought. Joan dashed over briefly to help serve up the main course - to make sure it was presented to her own high standards - then went back to oversee her crowded, convivial restaurant.

And all the time, we were racking our brains wondering how this mix-up could have happened. Mr Smith was adamant that a man had answered the phone and assured him that a table was available. Yet apart from Chris and Eddie there was no man who could have taken such a call. Had it, perhaps, been a woman with a deep voice? Perhaps someone had got the wrong date? Or turned over two pages in the diary? But none of the answers we came up with was entirely satisfactory.

Somewhere between the main course and the pudding, when the Smith party was steadily munching at generous helpings of turkey and Chris was catching his breath after making an extra journey to fetch more cream (he had spilt the first lot during a fifth circuit of the steeplechase course), he had a sudden brainwave. It led him to telephone the restaurant at Blickling Hall.

'How are you getting on with your Christmas lunches?' he asked Stewart, the Blickling catering manager. 'Did all your parties arrive? You're not, by chance, waiting for a party of six?'

'You must be clairvoyant!' came the reply. 'Yes, we've been waiting since one o'clock for them to turn up. Party in the name of Smith. He phoned yesterday. I took the booking myself.'

'Ah...'

It's an easy enough mistake to make. If you look in the phone book under 'National Trust', our number and Blickling's are right next to each other. A slip of the eye, or the finger, and anyone could get it wrong.

Mr Smith and his friends were tucking into their Christmas pudding and cream when Chris appeared beside their table, all mine-host amiability, hoping that they were enjoying their meal. They were. The sherry, the good food and the warm atmosphere had done a lot to abate their annoyance.

'By the way,' Chris added, 'we think we've solved the mystery over the booking.'

'Oh, really?' The celebrants were agog to hear the answer.

'Did you look the number up in the phone book?' Chris asked Mr Smith.

'Why...yes.'

'Do you think it's possible you dialled the wrong one? You see, they're waiting for a party of six, in the name of Smith, over at Blickling.'

Poor Mr Smith was mortified. 'Oh dear me. Yes. Yes, I could easily have...Oh dear. What a stupid mistake. I think we'd better pay for our lunch, after all.'

Mary Mackie - *Dry Rot and Daffodils: Behind the Scenes in a National Trust House.* 1994

The Diocese of Norwich celebrated the 900th anniversary of its foundation in 1995-96. To commemorate the occasion, the Bishop of Norwich The Right Reverend Peter Nott, spent the year visiting as many parishioners as he could.

This extract from the Bishop's diary allows us to share his travels during part of that busy and hectic year.

Christmas Time on Bishop Peter's Pilgrimage

Saturday 9 December 1995
Chris Poulard drove me to Haddiscoe village hall where they dressed me in a chef's hat with the pilgrimage logo sewn on the front and an apron and I dished out hot soup. Afterwards I had a good walk in country lanes hard-packed with snow and ice. In this part of Norfolk four or five inches have fallen and the snow is quite thick and freezing still. Chris then took me on a tour of some of the other parishes in his large Group, beginning with a Christmas Fair in the village hall at Burgh St Peter where young people presented a very amusing and well-written Christmas drama comparing the commercialism of Christmas with the gospel. A feature of this group of parishes is the presence of numbers of young people and there is a good youth group which was begun about a year ago.

After a brief visit to a market garden shop, we returned to the rectory for tea and I had a long talk with Chris Poulard. He is an able priest, ordained late, who has done a marvellous job during the last six years... He has part-time help now in the shape of Mair Talbot, and they make a good team...

We returned to Norton Methodist Chapel for an evening Service of Praise with a keen choir dressed in an original uniform of blouses, skirts and coloured silk scarves. Here again there were young people present who did a mime and there is a thriving youth group consisting of twenty-five or thirty people, which is quite remarkable - something I have rarely encountered in country parishes. The service was led by Gordon Spittlehouse, the Methodist minister, and in conversation with parishioners afterwards I asked one couple if they were Methodists or Anglicans.

Their reply was polite but firm: 'We don't really take much notice of that. Actually we were both brought up as Methodists but we all belong to the same church here.'

I also met a churchwarden from Fritton in the Somerleyton Group who used to live here and comes back for this Service of Praise once a month or so when eighty people regularly attend... I said how much I had enjoyed my visit to his Group some weeks ago and that I thought things were going well.

'Oh yes, it's not bad really,' he said - a typical Norfolk reply which actually means that things are going exceedingly well.

Sunday 10 December
At Watton Methodist Church we had a period of worship and a Bible study with a large group of local people, all of them retired...

We then walked up the High Street, where I presented the prize for the best Christmas window display to Kings the Chemists, sang carols with some girls from Watton High School and then switched on the Christmas Lights (not very sensational at 12 noon). This was followed by lunch with a group of friendly old people at the community centre, an ecumenical Christian initiative which serves lunches five days a week at £1.60 - very good value. We then went upstairs for coffee in the same building to meet local councillors and had an interesting talk about the town and its problems...

After a short walk, I dictated some letters in the rectory and was then driven to the parish of Ashill with Saham Toney, now a quite famous charismatic parish in the middle of the countryside. Martin Down is an experienced, highly intelligent and sensitive priest who is managing his commitment to renewal with considerable skill. He took me to a remarkable complex of buildings called 'The Old Barn'. A Christian couple had bought these derelict buildings, set up a second-hand car business and let the other buildings to three interesting Christian enterprises, which I visited in turn. First there was the office of 'Living Water', which organises the annual Renewal Conference at the Norfolk Showground - it takes a whole year to organise. The office is staffed by a part-time secretary and Stephen Mawditt... In another room I met 'Action Workwise', dedicated to helping the unemployed. They give advice about CVs, writing letters of application and interviewing. But above all they help people in this position to value themselves because so often, of course, there is a loss of self-esteem which makes worse the experience of being unemployed, and with that lack of confidence it is more difficult to get another job... The final visit was to 'Outlook', a new initiative in evangelism to the over sixties, run by a former missionary. She started from scratch and has clearly touched on an area of major importance and, given the changing age structure of society, a definite area for growth...

We drove back to Ashill rectory and with Maureen, Martin's wife, the three of us walked over to the church for evensong...

Thursday 14 December
Peter Taylor, the Vicar of the Necton Group of parishes, dropped me at Keepers Cottage on the edge of the village for a meeting called Thursday at Ten. This is a group of young mothers and toddlers who meet every week, nearly all of them regular churchgoers. Eleven of us, with approximately the same number of children aged between six months and three years, crowded together in the sitting room and drank delicious non-alcoholic mulled wine. We then sang Christmas songs and hymns, ranging from 'I'm Dreaming of a White Christmas' to 'Hark the Herald Angels Sing', interspersed with talk and prayers about Christmas. It included a little play in which I was given the part of an angel called Tom. The leader of the group then drove me to North Pickenham for a Bible study in a parishioner's house, led by Jeffrey Platt, a retired priest and widower who is full of exuberant energy...

The tiny school at North Pickenham consists of less than thirty pupils and I spent an hour visiting both classes and talking to the children...they were friendly and we had fun together until a churchwarden arrived to take me to my next port of call...

We drove to Necton Church for *BCP* evensong led by Peter Taylor with the churchwardens and two or three other parishioners present. Yet again when talking to the churchwardens I was impressed with the amount of restoration work that has been done and in a few years' time they will have completely restored and renovated this church to a high standard. I was glad to leave early to return to Norwich and catch up with some letters and prepare for the long day tomorrow in the Hilborough Group.

Friday 15 December
I knew that this day in the Hilborough Group was going to be one of the longest and most demanding days of my pilgrimage and so it proved to be, but with more positive experiences and a sense of God's grace than I had dared to hope for. I visited all ten churches in the Group and in each one we had a Bible reading and prayers, and in most of them, a talk with parishioners.

We began at Cockley Cley... One of the churchwardens of Cockley Cley, Geoffrey Crisp, faithfully says morning prayer in the church each day... The churches were nearly all pretty cold and Geoffrey Crisp, an old man, thin on top, asked permission to wear a woolly hat. I said I wished I had a purple one and would gladly have worn it too... Oxborough... Didlington...

We drove to Mundford Community Centre where the old people were preparing to have their Christmas lunch. 'Mundford Over Sixties Club welcomes Bishop Peter' proclaimed a poster over the door. 'Oh well,' I thought, 'another hour with the old dears.' And then I remembered I was over sixty, too, and qualified to join their club as one of the 'old dears' myself.

I left with Graham [Drake] for a drink at the Twenty Churchwardens public house at Cockley Cley...We had a good time in the pub before driving off to Rowley Farm, the home of Margaret and Sam Steward, for a light lunch...

Graham and I set off again across the benefice to W.H. Knights, the huge vegetable packing factory at Gooderstone which employs 8,000 people, and I had half an hour talking to workers on the assembly line. They are remarkably cheerful in view of the repetitive work and long hours, standing all the time. The workers travel long distances to begin work at 7 a.m. ... I called in at Gooderstone School to see the children before they went home, dished out badges and talked about the pilgrimage.

We drove on to four more churches, all with parishioners present except Threxton, where we arrived in darkness. It is only a tiny village with twenty-nine inhabitants, so Graham and I prayed by torchlight in the tiny church. By the time we returned to Graham's house we had travelled sixty-five miles during the day.

Saturday 16 December
A day in Swaffham began in the marvellous parish church where parishioners were decorating for Christmas and putting lights on an enormous Christmas tree. I spent the rest of the morning with two parishioners who took me on a tour of Swaffham market which is one of the best known Saturday markets in Norfolk, to which people come from miles around. It filled the main street, selling everything, and we wandered through the stalls... There was a bitter east wind blowing and I was glad after an hour to be taken to the Methodist church for coffee, which they serve each Saturday to visitors to the market. After half an hour we set out again on more tours, including a visit to the outside auctions of flowers, plants and ironmongery of various kinds. We met a number of parishioners...

By 12.30 I was frozen stiff and glad to be taken to the home of Rachel Wilson for lunch. She was there with her brother, a retired prep school master, and a friend. There was a roaring fire, sherry waiting and it was marvellous to have the opportunity to thaw out...

Sheila Nunney, the curate of Swaffham, soon to become assistant chaplain at the Norfolk and Norwich Hospital, accompanied me to the community hospital - a fine modern complex which is served by local GPs and is extremely well equipped and comfortable...

I spent an hour visiting all the twelve or fourteen patients. Following visits to two men, five minutes later their parish priests, Peter Taylor and Stuart Nairn, came to visit them and afterwards said to me their visits had been quite superfluous because the men were full of having had a chat with the Bishop...

I was glad to learn that the afternoon Bible study was to be at the Methodist Chapel Rooms. The Methodists always keep their churches and halls warm, so the twenty or so people who had gathered spent a comfortable hour in good discussion followed by a cup of tea.

Before leaving for home, I went to see Freda Blackburne, the widow of Bishop Hugh who died recently. We had a drink together and talked. She was tearful and cheerful at the same time... She told me she used the Pilgrimage Prayer each night and that it helped... But after Christmas she will go off to Spain to visit her son and is very grateful for the support of her many friends.

Sunday 17 December
After getting lost in country lanes, we arrived at Stow Bedon Church five minutes late. I was greeted cheerfully by a

churchwarden who, when I apologised, said, 'That's OK. We've been doing some hymn practice.' This sounded slightly odd until I looked at the register and discovered that the service was scheduled to begin a quarter of an hour earlier than the time written on my programme. So no wonder, with twenty minutes to fill, they had a practice... We had Prayer Book Communion sung to Merbecke which brought back old memories, and then we drove to the beautiful church at Great Hockham, set in a park and with wonderful wall paintings. Here we had *ASB* and instead of a sermon I read them John Betjeman's poem about Christmas, which I love and which I think people enjoyed:

Christmas

The bells of waiting Advent ring,
The Tortoise stove is lit again
And lamp-oil light across the night
Has caught the streaks of winter rain
In many a stained-glass window sheen
From Crimson Lake to Hooker's Green.

The holly in the windy hedge
And round the Manor House the yew
Will soon be stripped to deck the ledge,
The altar, font and arch and pew,
So that the villagers can say
"The church looks nice" on Christmas Day.

Provincial public houses blaze
And Corporation tramcars clang,
On lighted tenements I gaze
Where paper decorations hang,
And bunting in the red Town Hall
Says "Merry Christmas to you all."

And London shops on Christmas Eve
Are strung with silver bells and flowers
As hurrying clerks the City leave
To pigeon-haunted classic towers,
And marbled clouds go scudding by
The many-steepled London sky.

Norfolk at Christmas

And girls in slacks remember Dad,
And oafish louts remember Mum,
And sleepless children's hearts are glad,
And Christmas-morning bells say "Come!"
Even to shining ones who dwell
Safe in the Dorchester Hotel.

And is it true ? And is it true,
This most tremendous tale of all,
Seen in a stained-glass window's hue,
A Baby in an ox's stall ?
The Maker of the stars and sea
Become a Child on earth for me ?

And is it true ? For if it is,
No loving fingers tying strings
Around those tissued fripperies,
The sweet and silly Christmas things,
Bath salts and inexpensive scent
And hideous tie so kindly meant,

No love that in a family dwells,
No carolling in frosty air,
Nor all the steeple-shaking bells
Can with this single Truth compare –
That God was Man in Palestine
And lives to-day in Bread and Wine.

John Betjeman - *Collected Poems.* 1958

This was the end of the pilgrimage in the Breckland deanery because, as it is the Sunday before Christmas, the rest of the day in these parishes is full of carol services and it was impossible to arrange a deanery service in the afternoon. Given the exhausting week and my cold, which is still hanging around, I was very grateful.

Christmas and New Year

The cathedral services at Christmas were packed to the doors - there seemed to be more people than ever this year. In my Christmas sermon I read a poem by John Taylor, who used to be Bishop of Winchester. Called 'To a Grandchild', it is both beautiful and telling:

Over the swinging parapet of my arm
your sentinel eyes lean gazing. Hugely alert
in the pale unfinished clay of your infant face,
they drink light from this candle on the tree.
Drinking, not pondering, each bright thing you see,
you make it yours without analysis
and, stopping down the aperture of thought
to a fine pinhole, you are filled with flame.

Give me for Christmas, then, your kind of seeing,
not studying candles - angel, manger, star -
but staring as at a portrait, God's I guess,
that shocks and holds the eye, till all my being,
gathered, intent and still, as now you are,
breathes out its wonder in a wordless yes.

On Boxing Day I went to Carrow Road to see Norwich defeated by Southend. They are having a miserable time...

The weekend after Christmas was spent, as always, at Sandringham. It coincided this year with my birthday on the Saturday and New Year's Eve on Sunday. I missed being with my family, but I enjoy this weekend each year, which is a privilege enjoyed only by Bishops of Norwich. For the five weekends after Christmas a bishop is invited but normally only once in his period of office. This was my eleventh visit.

The Right Reverend Peter Nott, Bishop of Norwich. Abridged from *Bishop Peter's Pilgrimage: His Diary and Sketchbook 1995-96: A year's journey to celebrate 900 years of the Diocese of Norwich.*

Feeding the ducks at Chapel Pit, Hickling. Watercolour by *Eileen Mitchell-Kingstone* used as a Christmas card in aid of East Anglia's Children's Hospices

Town mourns as Tragic Events Unfold: Deep sadness and despair at Wells

December 1999

Thursday December 16
William Cracknell and Wells lifeboat station houseman Lionel Fortescue set off from Burnham Overy Staithe on the four-mile trip to Wells in a 14 ft wooden dinghy. They did not reach their destination.

Friday December 17
Wells lifeboat crew recovered the body of a man closely connected with their own station last night when searching for the two-man crew of a 14 ft dinghy.

Thursday December 23
The six-day search for Wells Lifeboat houseman Lionel Fortescue ended yesterday...

Friday December 24
Hundreds of people gathered yesterday to remember popular Wells father-of-two and boatbuilder William Cracknell who died in a sailing tragedy.

Saturday January 8 2000
The warmth, support and care shown by the people of Wells towards the families of two men lost at sea before Christmas was highlighted yesterday, when one of its adopted residents was laid to rest.

Hundreds gathered at St. Nicholas' Church, Wells, for the funeral of Lionel Fortescue, 64, who died off the North Norfolk coast.

"It brings home how dangerous the sea is and how vulnerable a community can be."

Wells Mayor David Jagger Saturday December 18

The RNLI flag flies at half-mast over Wells Lifeboat house
Eastern Daily Press

The Spirit of Christmas Present

From mid November 'Jingle Bells'
In supermarkets wails
To get us in the festive mood
And boost their Christmas sales.
And now the day is drawing near
Heaped high upon the trolley
Are cans of beer and cakes and crisps
And imitation holly.

Within this blur of rush and din
A face I seem to see -
A little starving desert boy
Who's looking straight at me.
Bewilderment upon his face,
And both his parents dead,
He sits forlornly in the sand
As flies crawl on his head.

Emaciated, bag of bones,
With sunken hollow cheek;
Though nothing's said we know that he'll
Be dead within the week.
He touched our conscience for a while
But news moves quickly on,
And though the starving boy remains
The TV crews have gone.

Unendingly and mounted high

The bulging trolleys come;
A pop star churns out 'Silent Night',
The tills at check-outs hum.
Then homeward with a loaded car
To gorge the hours away
In front of mindless TV shows
Through all of Christmas Day.

The vacant eyes look on at me,
So much they seem to say;
They hold me there, though hard I try
To turn my head away.
And as they look they seem to ask
'Could it be really so,
It was for this that Christ was born
In stable long ago?'

John Nursey - Silent Music

The Spirit of Christmas Present

John Nursey has published several books of verse to raise money for charity. He edited *Time Remembered: A Selection of the Writings of Eugene Ulph*, which is being sold to raise money for the work of Beccles Museum. Eugene Ulph's articles appeared regularly in the *Eastern Daily Press* and other local newspapers and journals. John Nursey is his nephew.

Michael Brindid was born in Hickling and spent his life there. Extracts from these letters prove that not every man is seduced into buying extravagantly lavish gifts for his nearest and dearest at Christmas:

"I Carn't Wairt ter See Har Fearce..."

December, 1995

I must say, if there's a time o' the year wen the missus is wath living with, tha's Christmus, so I'll try ter mearke the best on it while it larst. She say: "This year I aren't gorn ter be caught nappin'. I'm gorn ter git ahid an' not leave evrathing ter the larst minute like I did larst year."

She mearde har cearke an' puddins. She say they want ter be mearde a month afore yer earte 'em, she bearke fer the family an' fer people wot keep a-poppin' in.

I say: "Tha's a rummin yew want ter mearke all o' tha' grub." She say: "Wot yew wont ter remamber is tha' tha's more blessed ter give than ter receive. Arter all, tha' is Christmus time."

Enyhow I'm startin' ter mearke a short list o' things I're hard har say she want.

Tha's no good a-gittin' wot sh're alriddy got. She want a new skatt fer the winter, but tha' could be a problem corse I dorn't know how far round she is, an' if I arsk har tha'll give the gearme away. Then I dorn't know wot colour she want, so I think I'll give the skatt a miss.

Then I hed a bit o' luck. Wen she wus a-washin' up, she wus a-mobbin' about har ole fryin' pan. She say: "The time I spend a-cleanin' this ole pan wen I might be a-doin' suffen else. Wot I want is one o' them none stick pans."

I thort: "Tha's a good idea. I'll git har one fer Christmus, in fat I'll git two, one fer Christmus an' one fer har bathday on December 20." Now tha's wot I cal gorn the second mile.

I had a look in har cupboard. She hed three skatts in there an' she cen unla wear one at a time.

My mind wus mearde up. I'll git the pans. I carn't wairt ter see har fearce wen I giv' em tew har...

January, 1996
Well tha's all ova fer another year - Christmus I mean. We're had a nice time, though the missus say tha'll be a treat ter git back ter normal - wotever tha' is.

The missus was plearsed wi' har fryin' pan fer har bathday on the 20th, but a bit surprised ter git another one fer Christmus. I'd even put a bit o' pink ribbon around the handles an' wrut "All my love, Michael". She thort tha' wus nice.

She bort me a new bleard fer my bow-saw an' a gallon uv emulsion pairnt fer the back-plairce, so yew cen see how har mind is a-warkin'.

December, 1996
How time fly. Tha' dorn't seem a year ago wen I wus a-tellin' yew how I'd got the missus a none stick fryin' pan fer Christmus. Well, eva since then she're bin a-tellin' me wot a good thing tha' is. In fact she reckon tha's the best thing I eva did buy har, an' tha' she dorn't know how she eva managed wirrout it.

I dorn't know if yer think Um gorn ova the top ter year, but as I go round the shops I nuttice tha' not onla cen yer git none stick fryin' pans, but yer cen git saucepans, buntins an' cearktins. Did yer know tha'? So mer mind is mearde up. I'll git the set. If tha' ent gorn the second mile, I dorn't know wot is. Um sure she'll be suffin' pleased.

Arter all, tha's no good a-gittin' suffin' she dorn't want.
I're got a new pair o' shoes. The missus reckoned tha's suffin' I wanted on account o' my olduns a-tearkin' in water, but the nice thing about it is the missus bort 'em for me. She reckon they'll do fer my Christmus Box, so tha's me sorted out.

I know Christmus is a few weeks orf but the missus is a-gittin' excited about it. She like Christmus, allus hev done, so at the moment she's sweetness itself. Watha tha's the lull afor the storm, or watha tha's a-leadin' up ter suffin' remairn ter be seen.

I keep a-torkin' about Christmus, but I mustn't fergit har bathday cum a few dairs afore tha'. Tha' mean I shall hatter git har suffin', but comin' ser cluss ter the 25th is a bit too much.

If tha' could a cum the ind o' January tha' would a bin a bit more sense, but I can't do nothin' about tha' now. She're bin a-hintin' she'd like a rockin' chair.

I say, "Wot the flyin' dew yer want one o' them for?" She reckon they look nice an' hummly, an' tha' ud be luvely ter rock away if she wanted a snooze.

Arter spendin' all tha' on 'er fer Christmus I thort a bag o' wine gums an' a nice card ter mark the occairsion would be anuff.

But she'd got this all planned out corse the next thing she cum up with was a mearl order book wot somebody hed let har hev. She say, "Here yer are, tha's the one I'd like." I din't look at the bloomin' chair, I looked at the price onnit. I say, "I aren't a-spendin' all tha' on yer."

She say, "Lissan ter me a minute, tha's the price ready mearde. Tha's half tha' DIY an' tha' include screws, glue an' cullor stearne yer want. Yer'e bin a carpenter all yer life, yew can manage ter knock tha' up." I say, "Tha' ent as easy as all tha'. Tha' dorn't rock unless yer mearke it rock. Tha's like ridin' a bike. Wen yer stop a-pedalin', tha' stop, then yer blunder orf." She say, "Cum on, git it fer me. If yer loved me yer would." I say, "I'll think about it." She say, "Thanks everser much luv," an' gi' me a kiss on my bald patch.

Sometimes I dorn't know wot ter do fer the best.

PS Happy Christmus ter all onya.

January, 1997
I thort the missus managed the dairs a-leadin' up ter Christmus werry well. Evrathing wus warked out an' she wus in a good mind, that is until Christmas Eve. Of all the times ter lose the screw out o' har glasses!

There we warr, buth on us gorn about on our hands an' knees a-lookin' fer this little ole screw. She hed a magnifyin' glass. She looked like Sherlock Holmes.

In the ind we giv it up as a bad job. So if ova the holdy you see a woman about five foot airt an' grey hair an' a bit on the plump side gorn about wirra bit o' stickin' plaster on har glasses, lookin' like Jack Duckworth out o' Coronairtion Street, tha'l be the missus. Dorn't say nothin' corse she ont think tha's werry funny.

She wus plearsed wi' har bearkin' tins I got har, at least she said she wus…

The missus hed yit more tins o' talc ter add ter har collection. She say: "Wudder people think I dew wirrall on it? I powder all I're got, wot more can I dew?"…

Michael Brindid - Abridged from *I Din't Say Nothin'...Ag'in!* 1998

In December 2001 Marianne Gibbs wrote a seasonable plea for sanity to the *Eastern Daily Press:*

Happiness Doesn't Have a Price Tag

I am a member of Scrooge - the Society to Curtail Ridiculous, Outrageous and Ostentatious Gift Exchanges. Scrooge was founded in 1979 to provide good-natured moral support for people who want to stop wasting large amounts of money on Christmas presents that don't seem to make anybody that much happier for that much longer.

Members of Scrooge try to avoid giving (and receiving) extremely expensive gifts, particularly the heavily advertised status symbol items that are not very useful or practical.

We also make every effort to use cash rather than credit cards to buy gifts that emphasise thought and originality.

I would like to urge people to remember that a happy Christmas is not for sale in any shop, for any amount of money. Indeed, gift overload, followed by food overload, coupled with drink overload, is the way to ruin not just Christmas Day, but most of the New Year as well.

I'd like to wish readers a happy and frugal holiday season followed by a prosperous New Year.

Letter from Marianne Gibbs 18 December 2001 *Eastern Daily Press*

Sharon Griffiths too has had her share of problems with inappropriate Christmas gifts:

Don't You Dare Buy Me a Pixie Hood

On the first day of Christmas my true love sent to me...OK, come on, what would you do with a partridge in a pear tree?...

That's the trouble with presents. They're often not quite what you want...

The answer is what my sister and I have labelled the Pixie Hood solution.

This is because, once upon a time, a long time ago, a much-loved aunt

The National Shrine of Our Lady, Walsingham. The Crib in the Chapel of Reconciliation.

Photographed in December 2001

sent me a pixie hood for Christmas. It was made of white nylon fur and fastened with great big pompoms. I have never been what you might call a pixie hood type of person and the only good thing about it was that when I tried it on, it reduced the entire family to helpless uncontrollable giggles and added to the jollity of Christmas Day.

(Somewhere, there's a photo, but I absolutely refuse to go and look for it.)

The reason my aunt, bless her, bought it for me is that they were highly fashionable that year. Maybe it was something to do with the original Dr Zhivago.

Anyway, my sister and I decided that the best thing to do with Christmas lists is not to make a list of things you'd like - however appealing - but instead to make a list of things you really wouldn't.

Top of our original list of things we definitely did NOT want (It was a very long time ago) were nylon fur gloves, any record by Pat Boone, any book by Barbara Cartland and any perfume that cost less than 19s/6d.

But every year there are items in the shops that fulfil no other purpose than for people without ideas to give as presents. As they are often highly advertised and promoted, it's essential to spot them and put them on your list of things to avoid.

That way, you should be spared the real horrors, yet still give scope for nice surprises...

Just make sure that Father Christmas knows it's what you DON'T want. Otherwise Christmas morning could be a bigger surprise than you'd bargained for.

Even without all those partridges and leaping lords.
Sharon Griffiths 9 December 2002 Abridged from *Don't You Dare...
Eastern Daily Press.*

I stopped at the next town I came to. It was in a blaze of Christmas, with wool snow on all the goods in the windows, even in the wool shop.
Adrian Bell 27 December 1958 *The Music-Makers*

An up-to-date view of the rigours of Christmas shopping in Norwich is found in the pages of Raffaella Barker's novel *Hens Dancing*. Her heroine, Venetia, shops at Marks and Spencer accompanied by her pre-school age daughter. She also needs to produce an outfit for a seven-year-old Joseph for the school nativity play, support another son at his carol service, conjure up festive fare, act as canine midwife ... and still laugh at cracker jokes. Harassed mothers will admire her resilience.

The town full of Christmas glitter, and children having their noses wiped...
Adrian Bell 31 December 1960 *Flashbacks on 1960.*

The Spirit of Christmas to Come

It is traditional at this time of year to try to look to the future and predict possible trends. We know that technology is taking us into the age of buying gifts on-line, sending text messages to friends and relatives worldwide and ordering our Christmas dinner ingredients delivered to our door.

Electronic publishing too is a growing area and we can now access Christmas stories for children, Bible stories and sermons on a website created by a rector in Pulham Market. The Reverend Janice Scott has established *www.sermons-stories.co.uk* which offers free access to material to appeal to all ages. The legend of the Holy Thorn of Glastonbury can be read by people in all corners of the world and stories for children can be adapted to fit different cultures and lifestyles. A CD-Rom is also available:

Christmas Eve at Mangreen

Photograph by *Anne Reeve*

The Best Present Ever

Donny knew exactly what he wanted for Christmas. He'd been dreaming about it for weeks, and he'd sent a letter to Father Christmas asking especially for a Rocket Launcher.

He ran along to the postbox with his letter, and called on Mrs Billings on the way back. He liked Mrs Billings. She was terribly old and rather bent and she walked with a stick, but she always had a stock of sweets for Donny and she was always delighted to see him. He chattered on to her about the Rocket Launcher, and she nodded and smiled as though she knew exactly what he was talking about.

Donny had seen the Rocket Launcher on television and it was so cool. Donny had wanted it immediately he'd seen it, and was already making all sorts of plans to use it with his Lego and his favourite Action Man. Donny figured that by building a high platform for the Rocket Launcher with his Lego, he would probably be able to launch his Action Man way up into the sky. He could just picture the faces of all his friends. They'd be so impressed.

Donny dropped lots of hints about the Rocket Launcher to his Mum and Dad, just in case Father Christmas couldn't manage it. He thought he saw a twinkle in his Mum's eye, but he couldn't be sure. It might have been a tear; Donny didn't know.

On Christmas morning Donny woke up while it was still dark. For a moment he wondered whether he'd woken so early that Father Christmas hadn't come yet, but then he noticed the bulging sock lying on the foot of his bed stuffed full of all sorts of exciting presents. Donny could hardly get the paper off all the presents quickly enough.

He tore and ripped, pulled and struggled. Out came a notebook, pencils with his name on, felt-tip pens, a calculator, sweets, two wooden puzzles and a metal puzzle, three books, a GameBoy game, chocolate money and two CDs of his favourite band. Donny was very excited. He played with all his new toys until he heard his parents beginning to stir, then he went downstairs with them.

The main presents were under the Christmas Tree, and Donny's Dad read the labels, then handed the presents to Donny to pass round. Donny opened present after present after present. They were all wonderful and he was thrilled, but he kept hoping the next present would be his Rocket Launcher. When all the presents were opened and no Rocket Launcher had appeared, his face fell. But he saw his Mum watching him anxiously, so he did his best to hide his disappointment.

Donny couldn't concentrate on the morning service at church. Despite all his lovely presents, he felt in the depths of despair. He'd only really wanted a Rocket Launcher, and it hadn't come. Why hadn't God made sure he'd got what he wanted? All the other presents put together couldn't make up for not having a Rocket Launcher.

"Are you going to call in on Mrs Billings to wish her a happy Christmas?" asked Donny's Mum on the way home from church.

Donny frowned and shook his head. He didn't really feel like talking to anyone. But then he remembered that Mrs Billings would be all alone, so he changed his mind. He ran round the back of Mrs Billing's house, rang the bell and opened the door, calling out "Merry Christmas, Mrs Billings!" in the most cheerful voice he could manage. Then he spotted Mrs Billings, and he went rigid. To his horror, Mrs Billings was lying on the kitchen floor with her eyes closed. Donny thought she must be dead and his heart filled with tears. In that moment he discovered how much he loved Mrs. Billings.

He ran through to the telephone in the hall and dialled 999. Then he rang his own home and told his parents what had happened. They came at once, shortly followed by the ambulance. Mrs Billings was loaded onto a stretcher and carried into the ambulance. One of the ambulance men listened to her chest with a stethoscope and lifted up one of her eyelids. Then he winked at Donny. "Don't worry, son," he said, "I think she'll be alright. You got there just in time."

Christmas lunch was subdued, because they were all worried about Mrs Billings. After lunch, Donny's parents took him to the hospital to visit Mrs Billings. Donny went into the ward dreading what he might see. But to his amazement, Mrs Billings was sitting up in bed smiling. Donny couldn't help himself. He rushed over to her bed and flung his arms around her.

"Merry Christmas, Mrs Billings," he shouted. "You know what? You are my best Christmas present ever!"

Rev. Janice Scott. *www.sermons-stories.co.uk*

The use of the very word 'Christmas' is under threat in some areas. It is seen as divisive and unsuited to a multicultural Britain. 'Winterval' is suggested as a newly-minted alternative that carries no religious or ideological baggage. Will Winterval replace Christmas in Norfolk homes and hearts? I think not.

For Unto Us a Child is Born...

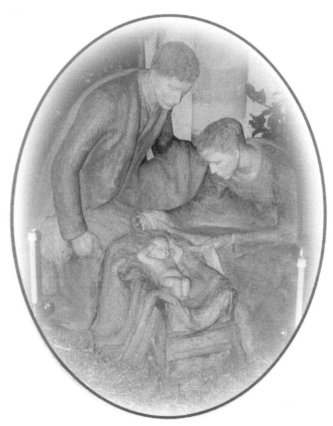

Norwich Cathedral Crib, by Josephina de Vasconcellos.

Photographed by *Patrick Smith.*
The Friends of Norwich Cathedral

The columns of the *Eastern Daily Press* play host to a number of writers on religious topics. Seasonal thoughts from a few of them are included here. We start with Advent:

Inspiring Words of Advent Anthems

I shall sing my first carols on Wednesday! From the platform of Norwich Citadel I shall lead the annual carol concert arranged by Activities in Retirement, which is supported by Norwich City Council.

This will be the 10th year I've encouraged our senior citizens to give it all they've got. They'll raise the roof, and we'll thoroughly enjoy ourselves.

But I put off too much carol singing as long as possible. First I like to savour Advent. These four weeks of preparation - like Lent before Easter - provide an opportunity to reflect on the wider meaning of the coming festival. The wonder of Christmas is heightened if we don't rush headlong into the kings and shepherds.

Advent emphasises the solemn side of Christmas. Peep in any church and you will see funereal purple is the Advent colour, signifying solemnity and penitence.

Before the gold frontals bedeck our Christmas altars, symbolising the divine splendour and expressing our human joy, some different notes are sounded.

Norfolk at Christmas

Among the prophecies and promises are stern warnings and talk of judgment - together with a clarion call to catch again the astonishing breadth of the Christian vision.

During Advent some of our most inspiring words and concepts feature in Christian worship. Those who don't go miss the lot! Here's an example - words from Isaiah set to music by S S Wesley and sung as a traditional Advent anthem:

"The wilderness and the solitary place shall be glad for them; and the desert shall rejoice, and blossom as the rose. It shall blossom abundantly, and rejoice with joy and singing. Say to them that are of a fearful heart, Be strong, fear not. Behold, your God! He will come and save you. Then shall the lame man leap as an hart, and the tongue of the dumb sing: for in the wilderness shall waters break out, and streams in the desert. And an highway shall be there. It shall be called the way of holiness.

And the ransomed of the Lord shall return, and come to Zion with songs and everlasting joy upon their heads. They shall obtain joy and gladness, and sorrow and sighing shall flee away."

The voice of the boy soprano introducing that final phrase, "And sorrow and sighing shall flee away", is one of the reasons I still believe in God. The effect is sublime.

The notes come straight from heaven-alone knows where, shearing through our intellectual pretences and our accursed materialism, and offering a glimpse of eternity.

If you don't know it, search it out. It may well help retrieve for you a rudimentary faith. Now that would be a Christmas gift worth receiving...

Reverend Jack Burton, December 7 1998

The Man Born to be King

In 1941 a cycle of twelve plays written by Dorothy L. Sayers for the B.B.C. was broadcast for the first time in Children's Hour. Each play in the series lasted for 40 minutes. On 5th January 2002 the first two plays of a chosen selection of eight, *Kings in Judea* and *The King's Herald,* were revived and performed in St Mary's Church at Tittleshall, near Fakenham, to raise money towards restoration work needed on the church and its organ.

The plays were read by Clare Le Messurier, the P.C.C. secretary, Christine Sproston, Andrew Edmondson, Tanya Ashton, Simon Fletcher and Anita Morling.

Dorothy Sayers' grandfather was a curate at this church in the 1850s.

Music, from Handel's *Messiah* or Bach's *Christmas Oratorio* to the most hesitant playgroup rendering of *Away in a Manger*, is an important ingredient of the magic of Christmas for most of us.

In December 2001 the former Dutch clipper the *Albatros* provided the backdrop to Wells-next-the-Sea's community carol singing event. Lighting designer Ray Lake, known for his displays at Foulsham and Holt, gave *Albatros*'s rigging a festive glow for the occasion and Fakenham Town Band provided the music.

The *EDP*'s Festival of Carols takes place each December in St. Andrew's Hall and raises money for charities.

"Many people remarked after the concert that the event marked the start of Christmas. It is something which has become an *EDP* tradition and we are delighted that people can enjoy themselves and at the same time raise money for two very good causes".

Peter Franzen. *EDP* Editor. 13 December 2001

On the Eve of Saint Thomas

On the Eve of Saint Thomas
So innocent was the grass
Of footfall, of nightfall,
In its silver rind

That it came to my mind
How rightful to consider
Is the date of Christmas
Between the first doubter
And the first martyr.

Shove, Thomas!
Push darkness away from us.
And pull, Steven!
Haul down more light from heaven.

So solemnly the sky
Carried the moon's majesty
Through a mist of hoar-frost,
As through a transparency

Of earthly-veiled heavenly,
That I thought of Our Lady
Being so far gone
That the child in her belly
Shone like the full moon.

Endure, sweet Lady,
To the end of the journey!
And yet-awhile lie patient,
O Maker omnipotent!

Sylvia Townsend Warner - *Collected Poems*

Better than the Christmas of our childhood was the Christmas of our children's childhood.

Adrian Bell December 1954 *In Search of Christmas*

Christmas Eve is here. The decorations are up, the school nativity play has been performed, the last card has been posted, the office party is over for another year, the shopping has been done, the gifts are wrapped and the freezer is full. It is time for the Christmas Eve service, whether we attend one of the Norwich cathedrals, a church, a chapel or some other place where men and women gather together to pray, or listen to the radio at home:

Christmas Eve at Mangreen

24 December 2002

During this year, we have seen many changes in our world, with wars and terrorism dominating many of our thoughts, but as we join together tonight, let our predominant thought be - Peace on Earth.

We all know the massive needs of the world we live in. We see every day man's inhumanity to man, and many of us feel that through our combined powerful projection of love, peace and compassion that there can be a positive way forward with a loving healing communion with each other and the world around us.

On the eve of a day set aside to celebrate the birth of a man, who came to teach peace; and a day for families to join together: Let us not forget those who are alone, homeless and destitute, the children of the world who are without love, and those who are sick. For many this day highlights their own hopelessness.

Let us acknowledge by our own words and actions a commitment to help alleviate some of the World's sufferings...

Let us send our love and light to all those who have died and those that mourn them worldwide; and may our prayers join all those that pray this night, magnified by the light of Christmas bringing a profound peace on Earth.

Let us empower the angels of light with our love enabling them to come on wings of love and peace as they touch every heart with a healing balm.

Closing Prayer

May the light you have shared this evening, fill your hearts this Christmas time with compassion, love, peace and joy. Take it out into your world and share it with everyone you meet.

God bless you all.

Maureen Harris. *Global Meditation Light Centre, Mangreen*

Christmas Day dawns…

Peace be to You
Peace to All
Peace on Earth

May Love and Peace Unite the World

There are many ways to tell the story of the Nativity. Margery Kempe tells us about the birth of Jesus in a practical way that is as far removed from *The Adoration of the Magi* in Norwich Cathedral painted by Martin Schwarz in 1480 as it can possibly be.

The Reverend Colin Riches, a Norfolk man born and bred, and for eight years a Methodist minister in the Martham circuit, tells the story in his native dialect:

That Speshul Bearby

Mary, what come te be the mother o' Jesus wus a young woman what wus a gorn out with a chap nearme o' Joseph; but afore they wus married she found she wus hevin a bearby. Joseph knew he wornt responsible, an he dint want Mary upset, so he say te har, "Mary," he say, "we better breake orf our engagement quiet loike". But durin that noight he hed a dream an in that dream an earngel say tew'm, "Joseph, moy man, dornt yew worry about tearken Mary as yer woife, 'cause that child she's a gorn te hev come from God, no one hint gorn te git blearmed. She's gorn te hev a boy, an umma tellin yew, yew'll call him "Jesus" what mean "Saviour", 'cause he'll searve his people from their sins." All this come about accordinlie te the ow Bible what say "A young woman'll hev a bearby what'll be called "Emmanuel" that mean "God hev come tew's". So, when Joseph wooke up next mornin he done what the earngel said, an arranged te git married te Mary. Then when the bearby come, booth on em got him christened "Jesus".

Now the birth o' Jesus happened loike this hare. About this toime, the Romans, what loiked everything writ down, got their hid man, Caesar Augustus, te mearke it known they wus gorn te hev a census fer the whoole Roman world: everyone wus gorn te hev te be counted. Now, this wus the fasst census they'd hed, so they told everyone te go te their own hoome town te soign the pearpers. So orf go Mary an Joseph up te Bethlehem in Judea. That wus hard gowin, 'cause Mary knew har bearby wus a comin on. Thare they wus, in Bethlehem, the plearce full up o' visitors, an try as they moight, they coon't git a room fer love n' money, 'cause, loike them, moost o' the people wus staying the noight: they'd all hed a tidy ow journey.

Norfolk at Christmas

So, d'yew know what? They ended up behind a pub in a cave what wus used as a stearble. An thass where Jesus wus born. They wrapped him in a bit o' blanket, and learde him careful on the hay in a mearnger. No one dint know narthen about it 'cept them animals what wus feedin thare, an him what wus born wus te be the Searviour o' the world!

But, howd yew hard, some fook come te know about it. A moile or two away, some shepherds, quiet, thoughful chaps, wore lookin arter their sheep durin the noight, when that fared as though suffun special wus gorn te happen. An, blow me, just when all the loights hed gone out in the town, the whoole sky suddenly come marvellous an broight. Now these chaps wore used te bein out w' noights, but, my heart, if they wornt whooly scared, 'cause they hearnt sin narthen loike this afore. But just as they wus all a dudderin, they heered an earngel say tew'm, "Thare's narthen fer yew te git froightened about, fact, umma bringin yew some good news. D'yew lissen hare. This very noight in this hare city o' David, the Saviour hev bin born, Christ the Lord. An hare's a soign fer yew: yew'll foind a li'l ow bearby wrapped up an layin on hay in a mearnger, d'yew see if yew dornt". Then, stret away that fared as though a whoole lot more earngels, loike some gret choir, wore singin fit te bust: "Glory te God up in heaven, an peace fer men on arth".

Arter that, them shepherds say te one another, "Cor, wha' bout that then? We better go stret away te Bethlehem an see wass happened, what the Lord hev bin a tellin on us". So orf they went roight smart.

Now, that so happened that thare wus some wise men from somewhere out East what'd come te Jerusalem. They say te Herod the king, "We're bin a studyin the stars, an we reckon that a bearby'll be born what'll be the King o' the Jews. D'yew know where he is?" "No, that I dornt," answered Herod. Mind yew, he wornt hev told them if he hed knew, 'cause he dint want anyone te tearke his plearce. "Keep a follerin yew them stars o' yers, an when yew foind this hare

143

king, d'yew let me know, 'cause I'll hatta see him too". Thass orl they got out o' him.

So orf they went, an that star what they'd bin a follerin all that way fare te stop roight over that stearble in Bethlehem. "We're hare," one on em say, larned loike, "we better go in an see whass a dewin". But just as they imitearted te go in, they see them shepherds in soide: some on em lookin at the bearby, some shearkin ow Joseph's hand, an some tellin Mary what they'd sin in the filds. So they wearted a bit 'til them shepherds come out: holding their caps they wus, and when they see them wise men they nodded respectful loike, 'cause they looked a cut above moost ordin'ry fook.

Then, in go them three wise men, an now them shepherds wus lookin over the door. They see them three with their jewels sparklin in the candle-loight, an they knew they woon't actin the part 'cause they looked se special. But as they watched they see them kneel affront o' that bearby as though that li'l ow boy wus more important than they wus. An then, d'yew know what they done? They see them undewin three parcels and layin them in the mearnger. An when they moved a bit, them shepherds see things what mearde em whooly gasp. Thare at the bearby's feet, lay a lump o' gold shinin loike the sun, an next tew't lay some frankincense an myrrh.

"I reckon we're a sin suffun special hare ternoight, partners," one on em say, "that bearby layin thare int no ordin'ry one". Learter on, when they wus a gorn back te their sheep they knew they'd sin suffun rare an wonderful what they'd never fergit. "Thass roight what them earngels said," they nodded as they walked, "'cause thass orl come about just loike they said that would".

Them wise men dint gorn tell Herod what they'd sin at Bethlehem. They went orf home another way, loike what God told em; 'cause they woon't called wise fer narthen!

Reverend Colin Riches - *Dew Yew Lissen Hare*. 1975

The Reverend Colin Riches now lives in retirement at Diss. His book *Dew Yew Lissen Hare* is worth searching for wherever local books of yesteryear may be found. This book has so strong a flavour of Norfolk about it that the picture of the shepherds and the star has a windmill in the distance.

My Christmas Wishes for You

May you find serenity and tranquillity in a world you may not always understand.

May the pain you have known and the conflict you have experienced give you the strength to walk through life, facing each new situation with courage and optimism.

Always know that there are those whose love and understanding will be there for you even when you feel most alone.

May a kind word, a reassuring touch, and a warm smile be yours every day of your life, and may you give as well as receive these gifts with joy.

May the teachings of those you admire become part of you again as you remember what you are receiving, so you may call upon these things at a later time.

Remember those whose lives you have touched, and who have touched yours, are always a part of you, even if the encounters are less than you would have wished. It is the content of the encounter that is more important than its form.

May you not become too concerned with material matters, but instead place immeasurable value on the goodness in your heart.

Find time each day to see beauty and love in the world around you and remember, what you focus on and give your energy to grows and expands.

Realise that what you feel you lack in one regard, may be more than compensated for in another, and what you feel you lack in the present may become one of your strengths in the future.

May you see your future, as one filled with promise and possibilities, and learn to view every experience as a learning and worthwhile.

May you find enough inner strength to determine your own worth by yourself and not be dependant on another's judgement of your accomplishments.

May you always feel loved and cherished for the very special person you are.

Maureen Harris. *Global Meditation Light Centre, Mangreen*

Epiphany: The Guiding Star is Common Humanity

Today comes round again the feast of the Epiphany, when the revelation of the divine glory was shown to be a gift for all nations and peoples with the arrival of the Three Kings, or Wise Men.

In the Epiphany myth, those travellers followed a bright star and, arriving at their destination, offered appropriate and symbolic gifts. It is one of those timeless Bible stories worth repeating constantly and perpetually updating.

We picture the Kings astride their camels. I enjoyed very much seeing the camels outside the City Hall at Norwich on the night the illuminations were switched on. The date of that event was far too early for my liking, of course, but in our modern society, religious insights have long since given way to commercial reality, and we either yield with good grace or get left behind.

The City Hall camels were a symbol and foretaste of the Epiphany strand in the Christmas story. To me, they were the very animals which carried the 'foreigners' safely to Bethlehem. They watched us with haughty disdain, yet something about them hinted at the grandeur and wildness of the desert. They should have been there this morning!

Several carols mention the Wise Men, but my favourite Epiphany hymn is Bishop Heber's *Brightest and Best*. It asks rhetorically:
"Say, shall we yield him in costly devotion
Odours of Edom, and offerings divine?"

Does God require gems, pearls, myrrh, gold? Then follows the verse which, with more simplicity and insight, comes close to capturing not only the significance of Epiphany, but as much of the meaning of religion itself as we are capable of comprehending:

    "Vainly we offer each humble oblation,
    Vainly with gifts would His favour secure;
    Richer by far is the heart's adoration;
    Dearer to God are the prayers of the poor"

It is all so simple! The heart of religion lies in no particular rite or method, not in rank or station, colour or class, intellectual ability, sexual orientation or any of the measures we employ to separate us from each other. It is about following the star!...

The Kings arrived after the singing angels had gone away into heaven, so probably they missed the divine music; but perhaps its echo lingered in their hearts, for there is always music wherever the star shines.

Reverend Jack Burton 6 January 2003

Deck the Halls with Boughs of Holly

The Holly and the Ivy

I remembered a particular joy in bringing in ivy and holly and embowering our rooms, when the children were small, and war ceased not by day or night even for Christmas...

Adrian Bell December 1954 *In Search of Christmas*

The Christmas Tree

The Christmas tree really is an ancient symbol, and not just an innovation of Albert the Good. Isaiah says, "The glory of Lebanon shall come unto thee; the fir tree, the pine tree and the box together." For "Lebanon" now read "Thetford Chase." And may there always be at least as many Christmas trees as there are telegraph poles in England's green and pleasant land.

Adrian Bell 22nd December 1962 *Bringing Home the Tree*

Hire a Spruce - and Let it Live

It is the season of comfort and joy - and the death of many Christmas trees.

Thousands of sliced-off spruces will turn from bauble-decked centrepieces of festive rooms into withered brown sticks bound for the tip or bonfire in the next few weeks.

But a new "hire a tree" service is doing its bit to stop the annual slaughter, and keep trees alive for years.

Customers pick a tree, have it delivered for Christmas time - but after Twelfth Night it is taken away to be stored, fed, re-potted and nurtured for the next year.

The venture is the idea of North Walsham couple Trevor and Sally Balding.

A keen tree grower, she had already built up a 5500-strong stock when her husband…suggested renting rather than selling them…

So the Baldings' business, Everlasting Evergreens, grows them in containers and delivers them, complete with care instructions…

Then it looks after them for the rest of the year as forestry fosterers…

Trees are tagged with names and addresses so they can be returned to their host family the following year…

9 December 2002 *Eastern Daily Press*

The Turkey.

The turkey may not be a native of Norfolk but as an incomer it has become a vital part of the county's economy. Viewers everywhere immediately link the words 'Norfolk' with 'turkey' and 'bootiful'.

Rearing turkeys was an entirely different game when Henry Williamson was a farmer:

The Norfolk Black turkey is making a come-back by popular demand.
This one reared at Langham Glass has no qualms about Christmas.

Langham Glass

Norfolk Tarkies

The time came to sell our turkeys. Loetitia had reared about fifty, some under hens, others under the hen turkeys, called poults. Four poults and a stag-bird had arrived in two tea-chests, perforated with holes, the previous February.

On March the 21st, the destined day, his four wives began to lay. They had made nests among the rising nettles. Each laid eighteen eggs, which Jimmy removed from the nests. Later they laid again, a second clutch of eighteen eggs. These also were taken away. After consultation with the stag-bird, they decided to lay once more. The elaborate rite of treading was performed. In time each produced another nestful of eighteen eggs. This third and final laying was untouched. The poults sat on them, amid nettles nearly three feet tall....

We kept the eggs, turning them every day, in an old German bomb box, which I had brought home from the Hindenburg Line in 1917... The first and second laying of turkey eggs remained in the box until foster-mothers could be found for them....

On Jimmy's suggestion a hen's egg was placed among each clutch, so that, when they hatched, a more vigorous leader-chick would show the little turkeys how to eat their food...

The little turkey chicks grew quickly. The danger was from wet and cold during the first few days of their life...

Soon they were big and roaming free in the fields and woods.

All during summer the turkeys wandered about the farm, coming morning and evening to their special feeding places. They could fly, and soon were roosting in the highest trees of Fox Covert.

Wild pheasants and half-wild turkeys grew plump...

The turkeys were brought down to the farm premises. Christmas was near. Some were bought by a local dealer; others went in rush-baskets to friends and acquaintances in London and elsewhere, ready plucked, trussed and delivered for 1s. 6d. a pound. At night, wandering round the woods, I missed the dark shapes against the moon which had been our 'tarkies' roosting in the tree-tops.

Henry Williamson - *The Story of a Norfolk Farm.* 1941

Parson Woodforde praised the black-feathered turkeys but fashions change and the white-feathered turkey gained the upper hand:

Turkey Country

A reference in a 1935 newspaper report stated that King George V retired to Sandringham to spend Christmas in his jubilee year in "turkey country." Today, the reference would be more readily applicable to the products of the private company headed by Bernard Matthews, president of the Royal Norfolk Agricultural Association. In that last jubilee year before the king's death in 1936, the Norfolk Black was the turkey linked to the county. As farmer James Graham recalled, his grandfather Frank Peele saved the Norfolk Black from extinction in the 1950s, when the rage for a white-skinned turkey almost saw the loss of this traditional fowl. Today, Peele's Norfolk Black Turkeys at Thuxton…is preparing for a third century of Christmas operations.

Michael Pollitt 29 November 2001 *Eastern Daily Press*

Turkey Farmer is Latest Food Hero

Mid-Norfolk farmer James Graham is one of the stars in the latest television series presented by Rick Stein. In tonight's programme...Mr Graham's famous Norfolk Black Turkeys are added to his list of food heroes. The Norfolk Black, which is very much the traditional breed of turkey, is a smaller and lighter bird with a "gamier" appearance and rich taste... Through the summer the turkeys are reared on grass and fed home-grown grain... More than 100 years ago, birds were sent from the family farm for sale in top London shops. Today, Peele's Norfolk Black Turkeys are also sold in the capital but a growing number are bought and consumed by local people. Although more expensive than the white birds, the traditional taste is a delight.

Michael Pollitt 31 October 2002 *Eastern Daily Press*

Feathers Fly - Far and Wide...

Norfolk turkey farmer James Graham is really moving in celebrity circles these days... At the BBC Good Food Show in Birmingham...he was virtually besieged by celebrity chefs inquiring about his feathered beauties...

19 December 2002 *Eastern Daily Press*

Before country houses had electricity they had fires worthy of the Dickens Christmas, fires whose smoke-flavoured hams hung in the chimney…

Adrian Bell *To a Poet*

When the Cromer and District Hospital was seeking to raise money in the late 1970s two sisters, Joy Scarff and Madelon Parsons, had a brainwave. They collected recipes from hospital staff, friends and colleagues and produced a cookery book. This recipe book was printed in Cromer by Cheverton and Son in 1981.

We include a few of their recipes for Christmas, starting with a traditional Christmas pudding:

Festive Recipes

Nanna Peel's Christmas Pudding

These quantities give 2 x 2 lb. puddings and 4 x 1 lb. puddings. Recipe may successfully be halved to give 1 large and 2 small. Puddings keep well, and improve on keeping.

1 lb. currants	6 large eggs
1 lb. raisins	Pinch salt, cloves, cinnamon, nutmeg
1 lb. sultanas	2 oz. ground almonds
4 oz. chopped peel	Zest and juice of one orange and one lemon
1 lb. soft brown sugar	2 oz. chopped nuts
1 lb. plain flour	A little brown ale or beer to mix
1 lb. best suet	

Mix cleaned fruit. Sieve flour with salt, spices, and ground almonds. Add nuts, add suet, add sugar. Mix well. Beat eggs with fruit juices, add zests. Combine all ingredients and mix to soft consistency with beer or ale. Three quarter fill pudding basins (greased) and cover with lids or foil. Tie basins in cloths if possible. Boil or steam for four hours. When cool replace foil (and cloths) and store in dry cool place. Before serving, steam/boil for another three hours.   *Monica Jacobs*

(Nanna Peel was the grandmother of Miss Peel who was Matron at St. Michael's Hospital at Aylsham.
Nanna Peel's name "wasn't Peel at all but I don't think we ever knew her surname! She was always known as Nanna Peel at St. Michael's Hospital where we believe she died in the Cottage Hospital, well into her nineties, while staying with Monica Peel." J. S. & M. P.)

Gwynneth Smith's Cromer Chocolate Crunch Christmas Pudding
(Serves 8 - 10)

If the family do not appreciate a hot pudding on Christmas Day and yet you like to have a traditionally shaped Christmas pudding with a sprig of holly on top, then this is a very good alternative. It will prove a most popular pudding for a family gathering of all ages and, best of all for Mum, it can be quickly made the day before.

6 oz. butter or margarine
3 tbs. golden syrup
8 oz. plain chocolate
6 oz. crushed ginger biscuits
6 oz. crushed plain sweet biscuits
1 oz. currants
3 oz. raisins
2 oz. glacé cherries - roughly chopped
1 oz. candied peel
2 tsp. ground cinnamon
2 tbs. brandy or rum

Icing and Decoration
3 oz. plain chocolate
1 tbs. water
1 oz. butter or margarine
A little icing sugar
2-3 halved glacé cherries
Sprig of holly

Grease a 2 pint pudding basin. Gently melt and stir together the butter, syrup and chocolate in a saucepan. Mix in the rest of the ingredients and spoon into the pudding basin. Chill in refrigerator until set. Then dip the basin briefly in hot water and turn the pudding out. To make the icing, gently melt the chocolate with the water and stir until smooth, add the butter and stir until melted in. Cool very slightly and then ice the pudding all over with the chocolate. When cold, sprinkle a little icing sugar over the top of the pudding (to look like a sprinkling of snow!) stick in the sprig of holly and press the glacé cherries in a cluster round it. Keep in a cool place, but not in the fridge. Serve with cream, cut into slices with a sharp knife.

Joyce Goodman's Overstrand Christmas Jewel Cake

3 oz. red glacé cherries	**Decoration**
3 oz. golden glacé cherries	3 oz. glacé cherries
2 oz. glacé pineapple	2-3 oz. glacé pineapple
2 oz. shelled Brazil nuts	2-3 oz. shelled Brazil nuts
12 oz. butter or margarine	4 level tbs. apricot jam
12 oz. caster sugar	1 9" silver cakeboard
4 large eggs	1 cake frill
Few drops almond essence	
12 oz. plain flour	
1 level tsp. baking powder	
6 oz. ground almonds	

Prepare cool oven 275°F Gas Mark 1. Prepare 8" tin. Halve cherries, chop pineapple and nuts for cake. Cream butter and sugar, beat in eggs and essence. Add fruit and nuts. Sift flour, ground almonds and baking powder together and fold into mixture. Put in tin. Bake in centre of oven for about 3 hours, or until cake is firm and golden brown.

To decorate
Halve glacé cherries, cut pineapple into triangles and cut nuts in halves lengthwise. Heat jam in basin over water, and sieve. Brush on cake, then arrange rows of fruit and nuts on top, and then brush with jam again. Place frill round cake.

Joy Scarff & Madelon Parsons - *Cromer and District Hospital Recipe Book: A collection of recipes by Staff, Friends and Colleagues of Cromer and District Hospital in aid of Funds for the Hospital.* Cromer, Cheverton & Son. 1981

And to accompany the feast we could have Norfolk Punch, Norfolk-brewed beer, Norfolk wine or Norfolk apple juice.

Christmas is showtime at Thursford. For thousands of people from all over England, and beyond, the Thursford Spectacular marks the start of the celebrations:

Festive Recipe is Always Delicious

A good few years ago I interviewed a chef, whose creations were marked by a lively originality of ingredients, contrasting tastes and intriguing textures.

I complimented him on these culinary virtues and asked where he had learned his craft. He laughed cheerfully. "I've never had a day's training or tuition in my life," he declared. "I started from scratch and went on from there."

37 CFR 1.1

He considered a moment, then added the clinching argument. "The great thing about not being trained," he beamed, "is that you don't know what you can't do - so you're free to use your imagination."

Now why, you might ask, did this recollection come back to me as, one evening last week, I was sitting enthralled at an entertainment which has become an absolute "must" in my annual Christmas calendar? Where else but the great Thursford Christmas Spectacular?

The link is that the creator 24 years ago of the remarkable Thursford show, John Cushing, had no more formal experience of theatricals than am-drams at school. Nor does he read music or, in the musicianly sense, "know" about the technicalities of arrangements and the combinations of instruments.

But like that aforementioned chef, he has imagination, confidence, a clear vision of what he wants, and a creative love of what he is doing. In short, like the chef, he consistently offers his audiences, each progressing year, "a lively originality of ingredients, contrasting tastes and intriguing textures."

Take the stunning effect of a major scene involving the entire company. They entered in solemn ceremony, in costumes which subtly suggested ancient religious ceremonial. To the accompaniment of organ and orchestra, they gave intense impact to the familiar textures of *The Humming Chorus*, from Puccini's *Madam Butterfly*. Suddenly, in a few modulated bars, this resolved itself with terrific grandeur into that great hymn to an English golden age, *Jerusalem.*

Quite simply, it shouldn't have worked. But it did, splendidly - all because Mr Cushing's intuitive sense of what will move an audience triumphed over the niceties of musical and dramatic theory.

No wonder that Thursford has become such an institution at Christmas time in this county, and far afield too. As I emerged from the wonderland of sights and sounds which are the essence of this special experience, I noted the ranks of coaches waiting to take their charges home - not only to local destinations, but to Lincoln, Hertford and Southend...

Charles Roberts *In My View, EDP* 18 December 2001

Christmas Cards and Christmas Stamps

Many churches, charities and other good causes raise money each year by publishing and selling Christmas cards. Several of the illustrations in this book started life as Christmas cards. Over the years Giles, the well-known cartoonist, (1916-1995) produced a series of designs with an East Anglian background for the RNLI. Giles is, unfortunately, no longer with us but Granny Giles and Vera are still raising money for the work of the lifeboats.

Moss Taylor writes an *Eastern Daily Press* column on birds to be spotted by sharp-eyed enthusiasts who are at the right place at the right time. The robin, fortunately, is less elusive and can be spotted in most gardens:

Season's Greetings from Robin Redbreast

I wonder how many readers have wondered why the robin features on so many of our Christmas cards? Previously I have just accepted it, but writing this regular column has encouraged me to research such questions, as well as many other interesting facts connected with the countryside.

The robin has always been held in great respect throughout the country, and there are many traditional versions of the problems associated with harming or killing one.

These have included a persistent trembling of the hands, sickness and even the loss of a limb.

The Anglo-Saxon name for a robin was *"rudduc"*, a reference to the colour of its breast. By the Middle-Ages it was widely known as "redbreast", the prefix Robin simply being a nickname, an abbreviation of Robert.

Indeed it was only during the twentieth century that the name "robin" was accepted as the official name for our most-loved bird.

As an indication of its popularity, it was mentioned by William Wordsworth in no fewer than 14 of his poems, perhaps the most famous lines being:
> Art thou the bird whom man loves best,
> The pious bird with the scarlet breast,
> Our little English Robin?

One aspect of a robin's behaviour, however, may not endear it to many people, although it is only following a human trait, and that is its zealous defence of its territory.

Although most disputes are confined to posturing and chasing each other, robins do occasionally get involved in physical contests, where the rivals grapple each other with their feet entwined and peck vigorously at each other's heads. These engagements have even been known to end in the death of one of the birds.

In autumn, young robins, unlike many other species, begin to stake out territories which are defended against other robins that may well include visitors from other parts of Europe.

Although "our" robins are generally non-migratory, those breeding in Scandinavia and central Europe do move south in the autumn, and some of these pass through Norfolk.

But returning to my original question about the robin at Christmas, one of the reasons is that early postmen wore bright red waistcoats, and were widely known as "robins". As a result, the robin featured on some of the earliest Christmas cards, and was often shown with a letter in its bill, actually delivering the mail!

Moss Taylor *In the Countryside, (EDP)* 20 December 1999

When I was young much of the Christmas mail was delivered by students augmenting their grants, and lifeboat crews delivered festive mail to the lightships. Manned lightships and students delivering mail have gone the same way as the $2^{1}/2$d stamp:

There used to be green Christmases, and now we have had a red Christmas. I mean all those little dabs of red that are $2^{1}/2$d stamps, which not so very many years back used to be green halfpenny ones, when halfpenny stamps were green. For $2^{1}/2$d it went to my heart to send no more than the printed greetings formula. Illegal or not, each card I sent became a fragment of a letter, since it is my nature never to see a blank space of paper but words, however trivial, suggest themselves wherewith to fill it.

Adrian Bell 30 December 1961 *Round the Hearth*

Christmas Crackers

Tom Smith's Crackers and Caley's Crackers were both based in Norwich.   Some of Caley's Crackers were even sold in boxes displaying artwork designed by the youthful A. J. Munnings, the Norfolk-born miller's son who became President of the Royal Academy.

Father Christmas

I once spent a delightful day with Father Christmas at Weybourne. I was recording a message from Santa to broadcast to children in the Norfolk and Norwich Hospital on *Hospital Radio Norwich*. As each train full of excited children steamed into the station the magical ingredients of a child's Christmas were waiting: the frosty air, the carols, the mince-pies and the red-suited figure standing on the platform.

In December 2001 the children of Acle Primary School won the *EDP*'s Ultimate School Trip to Lapland competition organised with Virgin Travelstore. They enjoyed reindeer rides, trips on motorised snowmobiles and a journey through the wintry landscape behind a pack of husky dogs:

5 December 1956 Caley's ladies making Christmas crackers in Norwich.
Eastern Daily Press

…And They Just Lapped Up the Fun

Despite the early start, the adventure began on the plane with a chorus of *Jingle Bells* to get everyone in the festive mood. For some of the children the excitement was doubled as it was the first time they had ever flown...

Of course, for most of the children the highlight of the day was…tracking down a certain red-suited gentleman.

Excitement mounted as we climbed on to motorised snowmobiles to begin the hunt...

The temperature was dropping and the children huddled together in the back of the carriages wrapped in reindeer skins as the adult drivers' faces turned blue...

Suddenly there were lights in the distance and something very magical appeared out from the darkness on the horizon.

There, waiting to greet us were elves, husky dogs and a welcome drink of hot berry juice...

Standing on the edge of the lake close to a series of log cabins, the children shouted "wake up Father Christmas" at the tops of their voices...

Another cry of "wake up Father Christmas" outside the front door and suddenly he appeared - larger than life, with a long white beard and a huge beaming smile...

Rachel Buller 18 December 2001 *Eastern Daily Press*

Father Christmas has been spotted nearer to home, taking over at the wheel of Mick Burton's First Eastern Counties bus, on the X94 route to Peterborough:

"It started out as a bit of fun and it's just nice to get a few smiles. People seem to love it. But unfortunately you can't have reindeer pulling the bus. Union rules say that they're not allowed to work before Christmas Eve."

19 December 2002 *Eastern Daily Press*

On Having Guests to Stay

The season of cheer, with kith and friends to fill the house, suggests the need for a new sort of guide: "Guests: How to Manage Them." When to hobnob with - when to leave alone - including a selection of Graceful Exits from the presence of...

Unpacking of course is your first escape from each other. Don't waste it immediately on arrival if that can be avoided. It comes in more gratefully after the first conversational spate... Big, soft, air-travelled cases of women are a good sign, being full of time-consuming trivia. Men's hard, shin-wounding little grips mean that the owner will be treading on your heels almost as soon as you have reached the bottom stair after showing him his room.

A warm guestroom pays dividends... Guests go up and nap of an afternoon, spend longer changing their clothes. A writing table encourages them to write letters up there.

The chief thing to remember about guest management...is that host and guest want to be apart for roughly as much of the time as they want to be together ... only obsessive types want to be talking all the time, and they need to see a psychiatrist.

Adrian Bell 23 December 1967 *Host and Guests*

The work of the Royal National Lifeboat Institution can take them to sea on any day or night of the year. Allan Frary, Coxswain of the Wells Lifeboat, recalls one busy Christmas Eve:

Service Launch to *MFV Toriki* - 24 December 1992

The maroons were fired at 07.15 with thick fog and a hard frost.

The *Doris M. Mann of Ampthill* launched in front of Boathouse at 07.25.

The only information we had was that the vessel was in shallow water somewhere between Wells and Thornham harbours. With visibility down to less than 50 yards we would have to use radar, but more importantly the VHF DF (used to home in on radio transmissions). By talking to the *Toriki* at least we had some kind of bearing but no distance.

The *Toriki* was being delivered to King's Lynn and had left Lowestoft late on the 23rd. She had engine problems (heating up), radar not working and the skipper thought the compass was out.

At around 08.30 we had got a good strong echo on radar and with visibility still down to less than 50 yards we eased in to see the vessel looming out of the fog.

Coming alongside one person came out of the wheelhouse. It was Georgie Fisher, a good friend and a well-known skipper in Lynn. The first words from George were "Have you got any fags", then "Gawd, I aren't going to live this one down". To which I replied "What the hell are you doing out here you silly old fool!"

After a lot of banter back and forth we began the tow to Lynn. The fog seemed to have got thicker by now and as we were just south of the Gore Middle Sand (a large sand bank that stands off Holme and is separated by a narrow channel from the Sunk Sand off Hunstanton) it was decided to make for the Woolpack Buoy and deeper water into the Wash.

Once rounding the Woolpack a course of south-west and keeping Hunstanton cliffs at two miles will bring you to the Sunk Buoy and then Lynn Channel called Teetotal. George was now on his own 'patch' and would call on the radio to say we needed to alter course one way or the other to stay in the deepest of the water.

While towing it had been agreed to leave the *Toriki* anchored in Teetotal Channel and when water allowed another Lynn boat would come out to finish the tow so allowing us to return to Wells.

The return trip was straightforward and as we neared Brancaster the fog thinned out to a bright sunny day. As the tide was out we had a low water recovery, meaning the launching crew and tractor would meet us in Holkham Bay, some two miles from the Boathouse. As the boat was beached ready for hauling out we could see some of the launchers had put tinsel around their hats and had decorated the tractor. Once the boat had been re-carriaged it was decided to break into the brandy that was kept aboard - For Emergency Use Only!

After getting the lifeboat ready for service we were all invited up to the *'Ark Royal'* where Roger the Landlord had got some rum punch ready for us. You could say our Christmas celebrations got off to an early start!

Months later I was talking to the owner of *Toriki* (I used to supply him with whelks) and asked what had been the problem with the boat. He said he'd had mechanics down to look at the engine and they couldn't find anything wrong. The compass was reading O.K. and likewise the radar. It has just dawned on me, while writing this, that George had been giving us instructions about keeping out into deeper water coming round off Hunstanton, so was the radar O.K., or did he, as I thought, know his 'patch'? My guess now is that he was using his radar.

An unconfirmed report from another Lynn skipper was that George had lost his bearings on the passage and had to make that afternoon's tide because he was due to go out with his wife on Christmas Eve. If the fog hadn't lifted it would've meant him getting to Lynn on Christmas Morning.

Although George is no longer with us he and I had many a laugh over this but I never did find out the truth. My guess is he just wanted a tow home to make sure he was there on the afternoon tide. I never did get the fags back either!

Allen Frary, Coxswain - Wells RNLI Lifeboat Station

At Christmas

Christmas Eve by the firelight,
The flames round the logs leap high.
I idly gaze and my thoughts turn
To Christmases long gone by.
I see in the flames old faces
Come flitting across the years;
Of loved ones and of laughter,
And burdensome times and tears.
But saddest of all that I see there,
As I gaze in the flames dreamy-eyed,
Is the face of one whose love faded,
And flickered, and finally died.

John Nursey - *Week-end in the Village*

How pleasant the hermit's life in mid-winter, provided the walls of his cell are lined with books...

Adrian Bell 10 January 1953 *Cold Comforts*

Making Paper Chains

Christmas is upon us before we can turn round, we complain. But it was not so when we were young. December 25th seemed a distant prospect when we came home from school about December 20th. It was unbearable to concentrate on Christmas Day from that distance, like trying to look at the sun. We fixed our thoughts on a nearer objective - decorations...

We sat round the table, making coloured strips of paper into paper chains, while Daisy, the maid, worked the gramophone. It played all the dozen records, and then we asked for them over again. The paper chains lengthened and coiled across the table and hung over to the floor. How tedious a task, pasting the ends of a strip to make a ring, and then another to link that ring, on and on. Yet to us how delightful, because of the colours, and every new link entailed a new choice. A green, a red, a blue - now, what next? There were some gold and silver strips, but not so many of these because they were more expensive, so we had to eke them out. But the satisfaction, when the treat was due, to make a golden link, and a little of the golden dust adhered to our fingers when we had done. Meanwhile the gramophone was grinding out *"The Turkish Patrol," "Soldiers of the Queen," "The Merry Widow Waltz,"* and *"Somewhere a Voice is Calling."*

Adult aid was required for the hanging. Steps were brought in which had a disconcerting way of giving another lurch when they had apparently been firmly set and a parent was half-way up... The hall, the nursery, the dining room in turn were festooned...

Christmas cards arrived, then holly, mistletoe, the tree... Then, on the Day itself an unnatural hush fell. The room with the tree in it was out of bounds. Nobody must go past the window even, while parents moved within, with murmurs and rustlings. All mounted to a climax.

Christmases themselves moved to a climax. The peak for us was reached, I think, on that Christmas Day when we were summoned to the tree by music, and found we had been presented with a gramophone of our own....

And then something happened to Christmas. No, it happened to us: we were growing up. Paper chains lost their thrill, presents became useful, and at last we even contemplated discontinuing the Christmas tree.

Adrian Bell 15 December 1956 *Christmas Decorations*

Words scratched in the first patch of drying sand

25 December 1999 Overstrand

There is something special about sharing a birthday with Jesus Christ even if it may mean that Christmas and birthday presents are combined and you can't have the mantelpiece to yourself:

Christopher Bush wrote under the name Michael Home. He was born on Christmas Day in 1885 and spent much of his boyhood in Great Hockham. He won a scholarship to Thetford Grammar School and became a writer of detective stories:

A Norfolk Boy Born on Christmas Day

Christmas would draw inevitably nearer, and in our house would be done all those things which you remember from your own childhood. Mother would be stoning raisins and cutting candied peel into the thinnest of slices, and we with our eyes on her to see who would be given the hard core of sugar. The time would come to help stir the puddings, and when the last available portion had been removed we would be allowed to scrape the great mixing-pan for ourselves and lick the wooden spoon. Mincemeat would be made, and ginger wine...

King's Lynn Ramblers walking on the Sandringham Estate. Festive walks programme 2002

Photograph by *Allan Jones*

In the week before Christmas there would be a special shooting party at the Hall, and for that week the Home woods were specially reserved... I can tell you that in that week's three days of shooting about two thousand pheasants would be shot. And after the shoot the keepers would make the tour of the village with Green's Christmas boxes - a brace of pheasants for a farmer and of rabbits for a cottager...

The great event of Christmas Eve was carol singing...

At about ten o'clock the singers would assemble outside the Reading Room and to 'them chaps' would be added the best male singers of Church and Chapel. The repertoire was strictly limited to five pieces: *While Shepherds Watched, Christians Awake!, Hark, the Herald Angels Sing, O Come All Ye Faithful,* and finally *The First Noel.* But as we knew only one verse of that it would have to be repeated. At each stop, two carols would be given from that repertoire.

If it was a dark night lanterns would be carried... In the Reading Room there would be a roaring fire to welcome back the party, but all along that route - not only at the Hall but at each farmhouse - would be beer and hot cocoa, mince-pies and sausage rolls, but as the night would usually be bitter it was the cocoa that would be most in demand.

Years later, when I was at home, I would lie awake in my bed to hear the carol singers. Each individual halt could be judged for the sound of the singing would come clear across the fields and through the frosty night. Then at long last it would slowly near, and then it would be beneath our own windows. Then it would move on, and it was when the sound came from the near distance and then slowly receded that it would make a kind of lullaby and at once I would be asleep. By then it would be Christmas Day, and it was on a Christmas Day that I was born...

Now at Christmas-time I was accustomed to chaff my mother about the exceedingly unpleasant surprise my arrival had given her... I repeated that now time-honoured joke and happened to add that it must have been rather nice in a way to have been having a baby with the sound of the carol singers still in her ears.

'But there weren't any carol singers,' she said.

I stared. 'But you always told me that I was born at two o'clock in the morning?'

'Oh, no, my dear,' she said. 'You were born at two o'clock in the afternoon.'

"Which reminds me , dear – how'd you get on in the city today?"

27 December 2001

Cartoon by *Tony Hall*.

Eastern Daily Press

'Are you sure?' I said.

'Of course I'm sure,' she said. 'Who else could be so sure?' Then she sighed. 'Wasn't I the only one in the house that didn't have a Christmas dinner?'

Michael Home - abridged from *Autumn Fields* 1944

Time for Christmas dinner. Cats for the last half hour have been doing square-dance figures among the legs of the chairs, and mewing, as the aroma of roast bird intensified.

Adrian Bell 30 December 1967 *Rest us Merry*

Christmas Day Service at Happisburgh - RNLI Style

Date   25th December 2001

Weather conditions   Squally showers, poor visibility
Wind   Force 6-7, from the North-West
Sea state   Very rough
Swell height   3 metres plus Waves crashing against the
                                                 cliff face as tide high.

Coastguard

The Coastguard Service called Happisburgh RNLI at 14.55 hours. A 999 call had been received and help from the Happisburgh lifeboat was requested. Pagers were immediately alerted and the lifeboat crew rushed to work.

The 999 call from a member of the public reported a dog in difficulties in the sea and people in danger. The tide was high, rough seas were breaking close to the lifeboat ramp and the Coastguard was afraid that people could easily fall in or be dragged in and swept away or become stranded against the cliffs.

The location of the dog and people involved was at the bottom of the boat ramp.

Coxswain
The 999 call reported a dog in difficulties and people trying to get it out in rough conditions. The Coastguard requested help as there was a danger of people being swept out to sea.

Coxswain and crew members found several people at the bottom of the ramp, all soaking wet and some crying.

The Hon. Sec. and some of the crew attempted to calm the members of the public and find out where the dog had last been seen. The rest of the crew had their gear on and were preparing to launch the lifeboat. Launching ropes were prepared so someone could slide down to the base of the cliffs, if needed, to rescue the dog or any person swept there.

While this was going on those with binoculars searched the sea and cliffs. Light was fading fast on one of the shortest days of the year. Time was running out.

The lifeboat was brought down the boat ramp and prepared to launch. Just after the boat entered the water a wet, shaggy and very tired-looking dog came running along the clifftop.

"The dog was a bit wet but all OK" stated the report, with typical Norfolk understatement.

The family, now rapturously reunited with their soaking dog, thanked the lifeboat crew for turning out on Christmas Day and returned home.

Nine people turned out for the lifeboat which was back in the boathouse, rehoused, re-fuelled and ready for service at 16.00 hours,

25 December 2001

The crew of the Hunstanton lifeboat often meet up with their colleagues from Skegness, just before Christmas, somewhere in The Wash, to exchange the season's greetings. But for Derek Fairless, Boxing Day 1988 turned out to be more memorable than he could ever have imagined:

1968 *Cinderella* at King's Lynn

Eastern Daily Press

Boxing Day Rescue at Hunstanton

I have really good reason to be grateful to the lifeboatmen.

On Boxing Day 1988, I was out in my dinghy when a quirk in weather conditions left me totally helpless.

I remember that morning being clear and sunny and the sea being calm. But when I was only 100 metres out, conditions took a turn for the worse so I decided to head back to shore, but in doing so I was caught in a crosswind which very swiftly whipped the sail across the boat and toppled her.

I was thrown into the water. Unfortunately, the centre plate was missing which made righting the craft impossible. Despite the fact that the tide was carrying me further out to sea, I realized that my only chance of being spotted by anyone was by clinging to the boat.

Thankfully, my wife spotted me and raised the alarm.

You can imagine my relief when a lifeboat arrived and hauled me to safety. Had I remained in the water much longer I would have developed hypothermia and eventually lost consciousness.

This kind of accident could happen to anyone - no matter how experienced or innocuous the conditions. I'm not a complete novice having previously attended a six-week dinghy course. Of course, we all think it will never happen to us.

All I can do is express my heartfelt thanks to the RNLI. They do a superb job and never question going out, whatever the time or conditions.

I owe my life to those guys.

Derek Fairless - One of over 120,000 lives saved by the RNLI

Morris men maintained a long-standing Boxing Day tradition by entertaining a crowd of about 100 outside the Swan Inn, South Wootton...

During their half-hour performance in wintry sunshine and a biting cold wind, a team of six from The King's Morris - led by their squire, Ian Price, and accompanied by four musicians - went through a picturesque routine of ancient English dances. David Jackson, their bagman - or administrator - who plays pipe and tabor, said the group was formed in 1978 and had performed at the Swan Inn almost every year since...

The King's Morris were collecting for Hunstanton Lifeboat.

Eastern Daily Press

If Christmas Day is for the Queen's Christmas message, traditional food and families, then Boxing Day is for sport. If the weather is kind a brisk walk in the country, or by the sea, blows away the cobwebs and encourages us to make all kinds of plans for a leaner, fitter year ahead.

Norfolk Ramblers' have a well-publicised programme of winter walks after Christmas to give us a taste for walking with a group and an experienced leader.

For those of us who wish to walk as a couple, family or small group the walks devised by Joy and Charles Boldero are an invaluable guide. Checking the time of high and low water in advance of this walk at Brancaster is a good idea:

Joy and Charles Boldero's Boxing Day Walk at Brancaster

This is one of Joy and Charles Boldero's favourite walks, especially at Christmas time when the Brent and Greylag geese and other water birds can be seen on the marshes.

There is a large car park at the beach at Brancaster. To drive to the beach, turn by the church in Brancaster off the A149 into a country lane signed 'To the beach'. The car park is at the end of this road. Brancaster village is situated on the A149 six miles east of Hunstanton.

This is an easy and pleasant family walk of four-and-a-half miles. Good for walking off the excess of the fayre eaten on Christmas Day! All the paths are in excellent order and well signed.

Directions
From the car park go to the road. Here you have a choice, you can either turn right down to the beach and turn left along it at low tide, or cross the road and the grass area and keep along the signed narrow path with club house on the right. Keep along this narrow path with the low lying marshes on left. The path widens with a path right going down over the dunes to the beach. If walking along the beach you will see a path on left at the end of the sea defences over the dunes.

If coming off the beach keep straight ahead, if along the narrow path then turn left along the high wide bank path, with the low lying marshes on either side with deep ditches. This path winds like a snake and eventually goes between trees. It can be muddy here after rain.

At the road we turned right along the pavement going towards Titchwell village. At the crossroads, with the old cross on the triangle in Titchwell, we turned left up the very quiet country lane. Near the top where cross tracks come into view and the Coastal Path finger post stands we turned left along a wide grassy hedged track which later becomes a rough track. There are magnificent views of the coastline and of Brancaster village.

The path descends and at the bottom of it, we went left to the road junction in Brancaster. We turned right for a short distance to the Ship Inn, then retraced our steps, crossed the road with the church on our right and walked along the Beach Road.

Just before the white posts we turned left at yellow marker signs walking up a track between houses.

At the finger post sign we went right, going through the iron barrier. We continued along this path which soon went on top of the bank back to the car park.

Map References OS Landranger 132 – Explorer 250:

772451, 767451, 765446
765437, 763437, 763423, 770424
772439, 772442, 771242, 772451

Points of interest
1.Walking the marshes area we thought we heard stints. We did see flocks of Brent geese. We also spotted peewits, duck and coot. If along the beach at the water's edge wading birds can be seen feeding, as well as the variety of the sea gull families.
Here, in 1949, a terrible gale brought the sea inland and it breached the dykes and flooded all the marsh area.
About a mile off the shore of Brancaster Bay lies the wreck of *SS Vina*, built in 1894. The aged vessel was forced into service during

the last war as a Naval blockship at Great Yarmouth. The *Vina* was towed into the harbour entrance and wired with explosives. Later she was moved to Brancaster, where the RAF used her for a target ship.

2. The village cross at Titchwell has a tall shaft with an expanded knob on top. It would have been used by travelling preachers, and is said to have been a stopping place for pilgrims going to Little Walsingham and the shrine there. Titchwell is, of course, famous for the RSPB reserve, which lies to the west of the village. It covers about 420 acres of marshland, and, from the hides, many species of birds can be seen. The reserve (01485 210779) is closed on Christmas Day and Boxing Day. The visitor centre opens 10-4 in winter but the reserve is open at all hours.

3. Part way along this country lane on the right is where the parish of Titchwell's nature reserve is situated. Butterflies such as Meadow Browns will be seen here in a few months' time, plus many wild flowers such as the spear thistle. This was originally a chalk pit, the material was dug out to build local barns and houses.

4. The Ship Inn at Brancaster is a popular place for food and in winter has a welcoming fire to greet you. The menu board is full of tasty dishes to tempt you. Charles enjoyed a pint of Tetley's ale on the day we did this walk.
The Bell is open on Boxing Day.

5. Brancaster is a pretty and ancient village. The Romans had a large fort here. Its walls were 11 feet thick backed by ramparts and a wide ditch. In the 3rd century it was a well-fortified naval base with navy patrols.
There was also a garrison for a cavalry regiment there.
St Mary's church is mainly 14th century; however, in 1960 a Romano British cemetery was excavated near the church and the Christian burials found were said to be 4th to 5th century.
In Saxon times King Edgar conveyed the patronage of the church to

the Abbey of Ramsey.

The lectern is an unusual one, and was given by the Sunday School children in 1912. The West Norfolk Golf Club gave the pews in 1904.

Joy and Charles's walks appear weekly in the *EDP Saturday Magazine* and in a wide range of books and booklets.

The Church of St Helen at Ranworth.

Photograph by *Theresa Bloomfield*

The Sales

Of a birth as of a birthday, the burden falls on woman… By the time the world half lifts an eyelid, the admen are at her again. "Hurry, be early at the Sales, Colossal Bargains!"…

Adrian Bell 31 December 1977 *Reduce Speed Now*

At The Sales

My wife said she needed sheets… I shivered involuntarily, knowing that the ice-sheet cometh, with its deathly glaze in the bed, against which hot water bottles seem powerless. But life must go on; and when, after 33 years (all but two days) of being married, you put your big toe through a sheet as you stretch, and the thing rends for the length of your stretch, you know that a new sheet is inevitable.

My wife was now buying a pink blanket like a dawn cloud… "I want a black skirt," she had said some days ago, "to wear with my red silk top."
"I should just like to see you in a long slinky black skirt," I said… "I mean, I think we should get some grace back into life after all that child-rearing, turning sides to middle, and the rest of it."
"Bless you," she said. "I appreciate the thought."

Flushed with success, I bought myself a green waistcoat at a staggering reduction.

"We've saved up to £5 today in sales reductions, and we've still got just enough change to pay the milkman tomorrow."

Adrian Bell 18 January 1964 *At the Sales*

Old Year's Night

A cousin arriving on New Year's Eve caught flu with almost the first breath she inhaled of raw (unconditioned) East Anglian air...

...The Christmas Stilton staggers on...
Adrian Bell 17 January 1970 A Long Quiet Time

When I was a child I was woken every year, just as the New Year was coming in, by the sound of dozens, if not hundreds, of ships' sirens greeting the New Year. I last heard this salute to the New Year in 1985, in Yarmouth, when there were so few sirens that the noise they made was only a faint echo of the joyous cacophony of earlier years:

Start the New Year with Plenty of Cheer.

Eat, drink and be merry - for tomorrow we diet. Last lap tonight. We shall see the old year out in style in the company of good friends, good wine and the last of the party food.

Then tomorrow it will be a lettuce leaf and a nice glass of water.

The Puritans have a lot to answer for. They tried to abolish Christmas, almost succeeded for a few years. They even considered Christmas pudding "a lewd custom" - so goodness knows what they would have thought of chocolate body paint and furry thongs...

186

But we do seem to have mixed up our New Year's resolutions with penance, as if we should feel guilty about the jolly time we had at Christmas and should atone for it...

January is long and dark enough as it is, why make it worse? Let us forget the idea of penance and concentrate on what we're trying to do.

Presumably we want to feel fitter, leaner and more at ease with ourselves and the world. The secret of a happy January is to give up the right things. Basically, this means giving up boring essentials but clinging to the luxuries. It's the only way to make life worth living.

You must, of course, eat healthily and sensibly with lots of fruit and veg. By and large I'm a great believer in eating what's available locally in season. It's the best way to live. Except in January...

I leave you with a final thought. A glass of champagne has the same number of calories as a glass of orange juice, and is infinitely more cheering.

Life is to be lived and enjoyed and not just for tonight.

Happy New Year!

Sharon Griffiths 31 December 2001 Abridged from *Start the New Year with Plenty of Cheer*

At a Christmas party the other day, we learned of a house so old that the ghosts occupied all the best chairs...

Adrian Bell 31 December 1966 *Ghosts and Appearances*

Old Year's Night, which some prefer to call New Year's Eve, is the perfect time for a ghost story. The village of Ranworth may be quiet and law-abiding nowadays, but once upon a time ...

The Wicked Squire of Ranworth

Every year on the last day of December an awful apparition appears on the Broad, and has been seen so many times that familiarity has bred a contemptuous indifference to it locally, and it no longer begets fear in the native mind. The story, briefly is this:

Colonel the Hon. Thomas Sidney, who at one time resided at the Old Hall, was a high-stepper in his methods of life, and was noted far and wide as a convivial and bibulous roisterer. His wife was a charming, quiet, peace-loving creature who, in her frailty, suffered with passive resignation her fate when she allowed him to lead her to the altar, and accepted him for better or for worse. Their early married life was fairly happy, in spite of one or two punctuations, which she quietly forgave.

But she had reckoned without her host, and it was not until some years had elapsed and she had presented him with a son and heir, that she had awakened to the sad but incontrovertible conclusion that her husband was a monster and that she had tied herself for life to the crystallised climax of a long line of hereditary drunkards.

He would return from the chase sozzled and incapable, with his horse bleeding from deep spur wounds and nearly collapsing from haemorrhage. He always boasted he could ride like the devil, and some went so far as to say that he *was* the devil. That he could outride most at the hunt was a fact, and many was the horse that fell dead under him as a result of his wild and inconsiderate contempt for its staying power.

Those who had seen him in the field galloping ahead of the others had often noticed a man in black on a large charger riding by his side, and when they had asked Thomas Sidney who he was, had been told to go to hell. The Colonel himself apparently had never seen him, or perhaps he might have mended his ways.

To torture a dumb animal always stimulated his appetite for blood-sport, and there was nothing he used to admit, that gave him so much pleasure after a long run as to come up with a panting fox that no longer had the strength to 'get away'.

The cruelties of the hunt he brought into his home, and many's the time a waiting-maid has taken the lash of his hunting whip which was intended for his delicate wife.

To drink himself under the table was a nightly occurrence, and, in his opinion, and I believe of most people of his day, this was a sign of honourable and noble birth. No gentleman ever went to bed sober. He was not only a 'three-bottler', but what we today would term a 'whole-hogger'. All night carousals were the joy of his brutal life, and his sexual appetite was a continual source of great anxiety to the families in the village who had female relatives employed at the manor.

He had no care or thought for God, man, or devil. He would hunt on a Sunday as readily as any day of the week, and on one occasion when the meet was held on Sunday morning outside the parish church, he cut the parson down with his hunting-crop for attempting to remonstrate with him and remind him it was the Sabbath.

This sort of thing, of course, was destined not to last, and his nemesis soon overtook him, which was only to be expected.

On the 31st day of December, in the year 1770, a great meet was held at the Old Hall, the greatest of the hunting season, and a hunt ball was arranged to follow in the evening.

During the halt for luncheon, which took place at the 'Rising Sun', at Coltishall, he made a drunken challenge to one of the riders that he would beat him in a ride to Hoveton St John, which would be in the direction of their return home.

They started off, and the Colonel, infuriated with drink and contempt for his rival, was making a bad second, when suddenly he drew a pistol from his holster and shot the horse ahead of him. The animal stumbled and fell, badly throwing its rider. The Colonel rode on and arrived alone, to the plaudits of the rest of the hunt who had gone on before the race, in order to be present at the finish.

The hunt was continued, and after a hard day's riding, they returned to Ranworth Old Hall.

The unfortunate competitor in the race was thought to have given in,

Felbrigg Hall.

The National Trust

and gone back to his home at Belaugh, but truth to tell, he was found the following day by the side of his dead horse, with his neck broken.

The banquet that night was a great success, the Hall being crowded with the members of the hunt and the élite of the countryside. Over a hundred people sat down, and the tables groaned under their loads of luxury. The place was ablaze with light, and the wine flowed like water.

In the middle of dinner, just as the host had risen to his feet with glass in hand, and was about to propose the first toast of the evening, a footman touched him gently on the arm and said:

'I beg pardon, sir, but there's a gentleman outside wishes to see you.'

'Tell him he can't!' snapped the Colonel. The footman went out, and returned just as the toast was being given.

'He says, sir, he must see you.'

'Oh, damn him, I won't see him. Tell him to go to hell!'

The servant withdrew and the glasses were raised in a shout of boisterous revelry.

Just as they had sat down, the doors opened, a tall, thin man in a close-fitting black robe rushed in, closed his skeleton fingers around the throat of Colonel Sidney, and dragging him forcibly out of his chair, lifted him up, kicking and shrieking, under his bony arm and raced out into the darkness with him, leaving behind a yellow smoke-screen of burning brimstone.

Once outside, the chthonic intruder, with his kidnapped burden still yelling and shrieking alternately for help and then mercy, flung into the saddle of a seventeen-hands charger as black as himself, and rode hell-for-leather down the drive to the Broad, where he galloped across the mere, leaving in his wake clouds of steam which shot up with a loud hiss every time a hoof touched the water. Away into the darkness they rode, and Colonel the Hon. Thomas Sidney was never seen again.

And every night of 31 December since that eventful happening, that huge dark horse with red-hot hoofs and its rider bearing a struggling, shrieking man under his left arm, races out of the drive-gates of the Old Hall, and scatters the steam and spray in its mad career across the inky blackness of that peaceful mere.

If you have any reason to doubt it…go down to Ranworth yourself, hire a boat, and moor off, under the pretext of a little fishing.

Wrap yourself up well, for it is bound to be a bit chilly, but nothing in comparison to the freezing of your *liquor sanguinis* when your Plutonic friend arrives with the man under his arm, who told him to go to from where he had just come.

So here's good luck to you, and before you attempt anything so hazardous, I ask you to put a codicil to your will and remember the Cathedral of the Broads.

Charles Sampson - Abridged from *Ghosts of the Broads* 1973

We may take this tale with as big a pinch of salt as we wish, but there is no exaggeration in Charles Sampson's description of St. Helen's church at Ranworth as 'The Cathedral of the Broads'. St. Helen's has a magnificent rood screen showing twelve painted saints, the *Ranworth Antiphoner* with illustrations including scenes of the Nativity and the Flight into Egypt, and a view from the top of the tower that is well worth the climb.

Ringing in the New Year at St. Michael's Church, Beccles

We climbed the belfry and saw the bells up-ended there like giants' goblets. There was an utter stillness, and no sound but of doves crooning in dim recesses, and the heart-beat of the tower, the deep tick of the great clock one stage farther down.

Beccles.

Andrew Dodds

A small window tunnelled through the wall gave a view of the sleeping town. Not altogether sleeping; every light was on in the bank... The pub, too, was lit up. Curious partners in seeing the Old Year out, Barclay and The Bear, both bright, one silent, the other clamant.

Beneath the bell-chamber, beneath the clock, the ringing chamber was almost cosy. There was a small gas fire... There were fifteen minutes left of 1956...

There were five men, three school-boys and two ladies. I noted that bell-ringing is graceful in a woman; it lifts her for a moment from her heels. There is recurrently that tip-toe lift and fall, as though she had just alighted on this earth... Down came the hands in unison, and the ten bells were fired together. "Fired" is the word. Clang. The Old Year was going. Clang. He's gone.

And now for the New. The peals wake again, smothering harmoniously the first minutes of 1957... At the fifteenth minute there is silence again and "A happy New Year to you all," say the ringers.

The town is black and silent, except for "Happy New Year" as the ringers disperse in a flicker of flashlamps, and their footsteps ring a last peal on the pavement.

Adrian Bell 5 January 1957 *Ring in the New*

Resolutions suggest themselves, moderate ones, suited to my powers...

Adrian Bell 2 January 1960 *Frost on my Tea*

Sheringham RNLI's First Launch of the Year
RETURN OF SERVICE (CONFIDENTIAL)

SHERINGHAM LIFEBOAT (under 10 metres)

Based at   Sheringham

No. of Boat   B536   'Atlantic' Type 21

Date of Service   01-01-1993

Cause of service	Person in danger of drowning
Type of casualty	Bather or swimmer
At Launch Site	At Search Area/Casualty
Time of H.W.	23.30
Weather	Fine & B. Cold
Visibility	Fair
Wind Direction	5
Force	1-2
Sea State	Calm

Which SAR Authority co-ordinated the service?   C.G.

Time

(B.S.T. when applicable)

First intimation of casualty and from whom received	00.29 C.G.
Assembly signal and by whom made	00.31
	Hon Sec
Launch from slipway or off beach...	00.38
Reaching search area	00.40
Leaving search area	00.53
Return to station upon completion of service	00.55
Lifeboat refuelled and ready for service	01.05
Which lifeboat official authorised launch?	Hon Sec
How did the R.N.L.I. craft behave?	Well
What became of Survivors (Person)?	Person seen to swim ashore and run off.

Please give here a FULL account of the service from the time of receiving the first news until Lifeboat's return to Station

At 00.29 member of public telephoned 999 to Yarmouth coastguard to report that a man had entered the sea near the 2 Lifeboats PH and had last been seen hanging on to the end of a groyne. Pagers set off at 00.31. Crew assembled and boat launched at 00.38. On scene 2 minutes later area searched nothing found. Established by local CGs on shore that man seen to swim ashore & run off. Identity not established. Returned station at 00.55, rehoused ready for service @ 01.05.

REMARKS, by the Honorary Secretary on this Service - Charles Hall

An excellent turn out considering everyone was celebrating New Year! Is this the 1st launch of the year?

Names of Crew	Names of Helpers
I. Dent	C. Ayers
C. Rayment	S. Wells
S. Neal	T. Simmons
M. Watts	P. Garratt

The RNLI is a registered charitable institution which exists solely to save lives at sea. It provides a 24-hour a day year-round coverage and operates over 230 lifeboat stations providing search and rescue coverage surrounding all the coastlines of the United Kingdom and Ireland. The Institution was founded in 1824 and lifeboats have saved well over 150,000 lives. The RNLI depends entirely on voluntary contributions for its operating costs, which in 2002 exceeded £282,000 each and every day.

Moss Taylor was out and about bright and early on the first day of the new year:

First Day of the Year Seldom Disappoints

I simply adore the first day of January. As the old year draws to a close I find it increasingly difficult to become enthusiastic about going out birdwatching. But come New Year's Day and I'm as keen as ever to get out into the field.

I suppose there must have been some starts to the new year that have been washed out by rain, but I only remember those when the sun has shone, and this year was no exception.

Despite the usual New Year's Eve revelries, I still managed to get up reasonably early and spent the morning at my "local patch" at Weybourne.

The weather couldn't have been better. Clear blue skies and virtually no wind, combined with a heavy overnight frost, produced a veritable winter wonderland. The crisp layers of snow that had fallen over the previous few days crackled underfoot and it was a real joy to be out.

Open water was at a premium, and an ice-free patch on the edge of the small pool behind the beach had been sought out by single pairs of mute swan, mallard, gadwall and little grebe. How the swans had managed to land in such a confined area was a bit of a mystery, and I also wondered how they would fare when they decided to leave.

Several snipe rose from the grassy tussocks, giving their typical rasping call as they towered away erratically, before dropping down again some distance away.

Offshore, what seemed like a long oil slick about 400yd from the beach, turned out to be a closely packed raft of common scoter, numbering at least 1000. Strangely enough these sea duck actually breed inland in northern Europe, often some way from freshwater, and pairs are normally widely separate. However, once winter comes they are highly gregarious.

Scoter are diving duck and, as if at a given signal, all of them would disappear below the surface together, leaving just a couple of swimming birds on lookout. Within a minute, all had bobbed back to the surface, when there was much flapping of wings, presumably to dry them, before they once more dived in unison.

Keeping slightly apart was a group of five velvet scoter, slightly larger and with a different facial pattern, but no sign of the American surf scoter that had been reported off Cley before Christmas.

Moss Taylor, Sheringham, 15 January 2002

I am a little frightened of the figure 1... It suggests, as it does today, a new start, with the implied injunction to those of us whose education was draconian, "Do better this time."...

This day called January 1 disturbs the figure of the year, and I know I shall be paying bills with cheques dated 1971 and have them returned to me...

Adrian Bell 1 January 1972 *It Comes Round Again*

Pantomime Time at the Theatre Royal

Every year my father took his children to the Kennington Pantomime. It was an act of pure altruism on his part, for he sat with his eyes closed during most of the performance. How terrible it must be - the thought ran through my head - not to be able to enjoy Widow Twankay. But one moment stands out. It was January, 1914: there came upon the stage of the Kennington Pantomime that year dishevelled men in crumpled toppers carrying lamp-posts: the music played, and my father suddenly sat up and roared with laughter. "A most ingenious skit," he exclaimed: "a most ingenious skit on..." ah, what? I have often wondered; I only wish I could remember. Something to do with Grand Opera, I believe. But it was above my head at the time, and I shall never know what caused my Scottish and usually depressed papa to guffaw once long and loud at the Kennington Pantomime. It echoes down the years to me: it was the last laugh of the long Peace...

"But when did you last see a pantomime?" A poser, that, from the youngest member of the household, aged sixteen - herself one might say post-pantomimic... "Well, isn't it time you refreshed your memories?" We took the hint, and the sixteen-year-old came too; but on one condition: "You are not to sit there making suffering noises, father."

"I hope they start with rhyming couplets," I whispered as the auditorium dimmed; "those are traditional." Yes, we had rhyming couplets, and a shoemaker straight out of Grimm. And whenever the story seemed to have been mislaid, along came the shoemaker in the nick of time, leading us through the firmament to Cat Land and back again. Maybe it was apocryphal to have Puss lose one of his lives at the hands of the Bad Brothers, but it was in the right direction of providing more, not less, story. It was certainly a coincidence that at the moment poor Puss was flung into the river, a soft body descended on my lap. I glanced down to find a real black cat looking up at me. "You'll do," his eyes seemed to say, and he curled himself up and went to sleep on my knees.

Nor did he vanish again when stage Puss was retrieved from Cats' Elysium, but slept on through abduction and rescue, through King's Palace and Ogre's Castle. He did not bat an eyelid when the Ogre roared. "Well roared, Ogre," I thought, and so did all the young. How children love an ogre. "Ooh, ain't he ugly!" cried a youngster behind me in delight. Are we spoiled by the wonders of Cinemascope? Not yet. A burst of applause greeted two magnificent pasteboard horses drawing the King's pasteboard coach - as also the minions of the Ogre who were the chorus in silver cloaks. While there went up a roar for Simple Simon at the last, who had entertained us with an india-rubber energy, not only during the scenes, but while they were being changed. At times he made a sort of speechless gobbling, like a Norfolk turkey; and for that he spoke with a Norfolk accent he was doubly acceptable.

Simple Simon's assertion that three times three was eleven drew a howl of derision from every child in the audience.

Perhaps pantomime ideally is provincial. For participation by the audience is a feature of it. When the King tries to conjure some unpronounceable place-name, boggles twice, and capitulates with "Diss," everybody is delighted. And a clown's attempts to cope with a stage cow are better appreciated, I think, a few hundred yards from a real cattle market than in the purlieus of Drury Lane...

But there was one thorough little urbanite behind me. "Is that really how they milk a cow, mum?" he asked as Simple Simon worked its tail like a pump handle. And during the interval, when a picture of a footballer shooting a goal was flashed on the curtain to advertise somebody's beer, "Is that City, dad?" came the awed whisper...

Audience participation was more uninhibited in Norwich than I remember it in London. Particularly the children's participation. Light from the stage glanced on cheeks and chins. All were working; those that were not singing were eating. And meanwhile soot-black puss not in boots slept on my lap. What a piece of luck for New Year's Day.

Adrian Bell 8 January 1955 *Puss, Puss*

January 2 Booking begins for the next Thursford Spectacular

"Bye bye Christmas tree... and hideous tie from mother-in-law...and ghastly socks from aunty Ivy...and hideous jumper from sister-in-law...and ghastly woolen hat from..."

Cartoon by Tony Hall

Eastern Daily Press **4 January** 2001

Holly

Twelfth Night has gone, and the Christmas decorations are packed away, but what did we all do with the holly when it was taken down?

It is interesting to note how many different and totally contradictory superstitions there are concerning holly. For example, if used as a church decoration it was thought to be essential that every scrap should be recovered by Candlemas. Should even one berry be left on a pew after this date, it would surely bring death to whoever frequented that seat.

If used in the house, it was often believed that, should any remain after Twelfth Night, every maiden in the house would suffer a misfortune or be haunted by evil spirits. The holly sprays were therefore usually burned to make certain this could not happen.

But this is a problem, for there were many who believed that Shrove Tuesday pancakes should be cooked over a fire of the Christmas holly, or that the holly should be kept until the following Christmas, and failure to do this would bring about a death in the family.

So now we have established when to take the holly out. But when should we bring it in? There are still many households, mine included, brought up with the belief that holly does not come indoors until Christmas Eve…

There are many who obviously do not share this belief, for markets are busy with the sale of holly from early December onwards. This marked divergence of beliefs no doubt stems from the long history of the use of holly for decoration and celebration. Each controlling body it encountered through the ages tended to treat it differently from that which went before, and a mix of memories has remained.

Early Christians adopted the Roman practice of using holly decorations and sending boughs to friends during festivals, and so it has continued. In 1598, it was written that every house, church, market place and street corner was decorated with holly at Christmas. By 1851 it was calculated that 250,000 bunches were sold in London alone.

Traditionally it was the men who picked the holly and decorated the houses…for a lady in a long skirt standing over a fireplace to hang up holly would have posed a considerable fire risk.

Grace Corne, Sisland 6 January 2002

And so we start another year, filled with good intentions and a determination to do better this time round. We'll just finish off the last slice or two of the Christmas cake first…

Acknowledgements

I would like to thank the following individuals and organisations for permission to reproduce copyright material:

James Ruddy, Deputy Editor, for permission to reprint material from *The Eastern Daily Press*;
Susanna Pinney for specialist information about Sylvia Townsend Warner and for help and advice;
Michael Schmidt & Carcanet Press Limited for *Eclogue* by Sylvia Townsend Warner from *Collected Poems*;
The Nativity from *The Book of Margery Kempe* (1965), translated by B.A. Windeatt and published by Penguin Classics. Copyright B.A. Windeatt, 1965;
Robert Sackville West for *Letters of the Paston Family* from *Private Life in the Fifteenth Century: Illustrated Letters of The Paston Family*, edited by Roger Virgoe and published by Toucan Books Ltd;
The Eastern Daily Press for *Parson Woodforde's frolic for Christmas* by Eric Fowler (2000);
Ron Fiske for specialist information about Nelson;
Greenhill Books for *The Norfolk Hero: Vice-Admiral Horatio, Lord Nelson* by Carola Oman from *Nelson* (1996);
HarperCollins*Publishers* for *Christmas 1909: Flashman at Sandringham* by George MacDonald Fraser from *Mr American* (1980), published by HarperCollins;
Bronson Fargo, Chairman of Happisburgh Lifeboat Station RNLI Branch for *Happisburgh Lifeboat* by Nicholas Leach from *The Happisburgh Lifeboats* (1999), published by Norfolk & Suffolk Research Group;
Anne Williamson, Manager, Henry Williamson Literary Estate for *A Vision of Christmas: Christmas 1914* by Henry Williamson from *The Story of a Norfolk Farm* (1941, 1986), published by Faber & Faber & Clive Holloway Books. Copyright Henry Williamson Literary Estate;
The Eastern Daily Press for *A Sprig of Holly: Christmas 1918* by Adrian Bell (1966);
Robert Bagshaw for *The Sad Tale of Humpty Dumpty* from *Poppies to Paston* (1986), published by Geo. R. Reeve Ltd.;
David Higham Associates Limited for *Old Year's Night at Fenchurch St. Paul* by Dorothy L. Sayers from *The Nine Tailors* (1934), published by Hodder & Stoughton;
Mrs Hilda Jolly and Peter Stibbons for *The Worst Trip that Henry Blogg ever made* by Cyril Jolly from *Henry Blogg of Cromer: The Greatest of the Lifeboat-men* (1958 London: Harrap), 2002, reprinted by Poppyland Publishing;
Philippa Scott for *Peter Scott and Kazarka* by Peter Scott from *The Eye of the Wind* (1961), published by Hodder & Stoughton;
Henry Williamson Literary Estate for *The Williamson Family's Christmas at Stiffkey* from *The Story of a Norfolk Farm*. Copyright Henry Williamson Literary Estate;
Mrs Nada Cheyne and A.P. Watt Ltd. for *A Wartime Christmas beside the River Waveney* by Lilias Rider Haggard from *A Country Scrap-book* (1950), published by Faber & Faber;

Norfolk at Christmas

Christmas Eve at St. Michael's Church, Barton Turf by William Rivière from *Watercolour Sky* (1990). Reproduced by permission of Hodder & Stoughton Limited; *Winter at Great Eye Folly, Salthouse*: Extracts from THE DIARIES OF SYLVIA TOWNSEND WARNER published by Chatto & Windus. Used by permission of The Random House Group Limited;

The Eastern Daily Press for *A Countryman's Christmas Notebooks 1953-1977* by Adrian Bell (1953-77);

David Higham Associates for *"It was a house that lent itself to Christmas"*: *Edward Seago and the Dutch House, Ludham* by Jean Goodman from *Edward Seago: The Other Side of the Canvas* (1990), published by Jarrold Publishing;

David Chaffe for *Tiki - The Wanderer* from *Stormforce* (1999), published by Stormforce Publications;

The Orion Publishing Group Ltd. for *All Part of the Service: Behind the Scenes in a National Trust Restaurant* by Mary Mackie from *Dry Rot and Daffodils: Behind the Scenes in a National Trust House* (1994), published by Victor Gollancz;

Canterbury Press for *Christmas Time on Bishop Peter's Pilgrimage* by The Right Reverend Peter Nott, Bishop of Norwich from *Bishop Peter's Pilgrimage: His Diary and Sketchbook 1995-96: A Year's Journey to celebrate 900 years of the Diocese of Norwich* (1996);

John Murray (Publishers) Ltd. for *Christmas* by John Betjeman from *Collected Poems* (1958);

Coxswain Allen Frary, Wells RNLI Lifeboat Station, and *The Eastern Daily Press* for *Town Mourns as Tragic Events Unfold: Deep Sadness and Despair at Wells* (1999-2000);

John Nursey for *The Spirit of Christmas Present* from *Silent Music*, published by John Nursey;

Mrs Norah Brindid for *"I Carn't Wairt ter See Har Fearce..."* by Michael Brindid from *I Din't Say Nothin'...Ag'in! Norfolk Dialect Letters* (1998), published by N. Brindid;

Marianne Gibbs and *The Eastern Daily Press* for *Happiness Doesn't Have a Price Tag;* Sharon Griffiths and *The Eastern Daily Press* for *Don't You Dare Buy Me a Pixie Hood;*

Rev. Janice Scott, for *The Best Present Ever* the from *www.sermons-stories.co.uk;*

Rev. Jack Burton and *The Eastern Daily Press* for *Inspiring Words of Advent Anthems* (1998);

Michael Schmidt & Carcanet Press Limited for *On the Eve of Saint Thomas* by Sylvia Townsend Warner from *Collected Poems;*

Maureen Harris for *Christmas Eve at Mangreen*, (2002);

Rev. Colin Riches & George Nobbs for *That Speshul Bearby* from *Dew Yew Lissen Hare* (1975), published by George Nobbs Publishing;

Maureen Harris for *My Christmas Wishes for you*, Global Meditation Light Centre, Mangreen (2002);

Rev. Jack Burton and *The Eastern Daily Press* for *The Guiding Star is Common Humanity* (2003);

The Eastern Daily Press for *Hire a Spruce – and Let it Live* (2002);

Henry Williamson Literary Estate for *Norfolk Tarkies* from *The Story of a Norfolk Farm*. Copyright Henry Williamson Literary Estate;

The Eastern Daily Press for *Turkey Country* and *Turkey Farmer is Latest Food Hero* by Michael Pollitt (2001,2002);

Joy Scarff & Madelon Parsons for *Festive Recipes* from *Cromer and District Hospital Recipe Book: A collection of recipes by Staff, in aid of Funds for the Hospital* (1981), published by Cheverton & Son;

The Eastern Daily Press for *Festive Recipe is Always Delicious* by Charles Roberts (2001);

Moss Taylor and *The Eastern Daily Press* for *Season's Greetings from Robin Redbreast* (1999);

The Eastern Daily Press for *...And They Just Lapped Up the Fun* by Rachel Buller (2001);

The Eastern Daily Press for *On Having Guests to Stay* by Adrian Bell (1967);

Allen Frary, for *Service Launch to MFV Toriki*;

John Nursey for *At Christmas* from *Week-end in the Village*, published by John Nursey;

The Eastern Daily Press for *Making Paper Chains* by Adrian Bell from *Christmas Decorations* (1956);

Bronson Fargo, for *Christmas Day Service at Happisburgh - RNLI style*;

Joy & Charles Boldero for *Joy and Charles Boldero's Boxing Day Walk at Brancaster* (2003);

David Harrison, RNLI Station Honorary Secretary, for *Boxing Day Rescue at Hunstanton* from RNLI publicity leaflet;

The Eastern Daily Press for *At the Sales* by Adrian Bell (1964);

Sharon Griffiths and *The Eastern Daily Press* for *Start the New Year with Plenty of Cheer* (2001);

Jamie Campbell & Hamilton Publications Ltd. for *The Wicked Squire of Ranworth* by Charles Sampson from *Ghosts of the Broads* (1973, 2003);

The Eastern Daily Press for *Ringing in the New Year at St. Michael's Church, Beccles* by Adrian Bell from *Ring in the New* (1957);

Brian Farrow, RNLI Honorary Secretary, for *Sheringham RNLI's First Launch of the Year*;

Moss Taylor and *The Eastern Daily Press* for *First Day of the Year Seldom Disappoints* (2002);

The Eastern Daily Press for *Pantomime Time at the Theatre Royal* by Adrian Bell from *Puss, Puss* (1955);

The Eastern Daily Press for *Holly* by Grace Corne (2002);

Norfolk at Christmas

I would like to thank the following individuals and organisations for permission to reproduce photographs and other copyright illustrative material:

Bryn Colton, Picture Editor Eastern Daily Press, for permission to reprint material from *The Eastern Daily Press*;
Norwich Cathedral Chapter Library & Brenda Lemon for articles & illustrative material.
Cover photograph: Brian Chambers and the North Norfolk Railway for The Poppy Line's *Santa Special* photographed by Brian Chambers;
The Friends of Norwich Cathedral for *The Adoration of the Infant Christ by the Magi* by Martin Schwarz, (1480) and *The Flight into Egypt* photographed by Julia Hedgeco;
The Friends of Norwich Cathedral for *The Nativity*, 15th century roof boss from the North Transept, Norwich Cathedral, photographed by Julia Hedgecoe;
The Friends of Norwich Cathedral for *Norwich Cathedral from the Upper Green*, photographed by Deirdre Grierson;
Andrew Dodds for *Snow scene at Parson Woodforde's church at Weston Longville*;
The Eastern Daily Press for *Christmas decorations Wolferton Station*, "They reached the royal station in mid-afternoon...";
The Eastern Daily Press for *Mulbarton School's Nativity play in 1965*;
Adrian Vicary & *The Maritime Photo Library*, Cromer for *Henry Blogg of Cromer*, photographed on the 18th March 1940 by the late P. A. Vicary;
The Eastern Daily Press for *Diss Mere, Christmas 1971;*
Andrew Dodds for *Christmas trees and coloured lights...in Diss*;
Andrew Dodds for *Market Place at Aylsham...Christmas trees and market stalls*;
The Eastern Daily Press for *King's Lynn Shopping Centre 1971*;
The Eastern Daily Press for *Norwich Civic Carol Concert...City Hall, December 1960*;
Mrs Peter Seymour for *Festive sparkle at Womack Water, a scene from Edward Seago's garden*.
Rev. Philip Norwood for *St. Nicholas' Church, Blakeney* painted by Derek Essex;
The Eastern Daily Press for *Christmas at North Lynn Over 60s Christmas party 1971*;
Norah Brindid for *Feeding the ducks at Chapel Pit, Hickling*, by Eileen Mitchell-Kingstone;
The Eastern Daily Press for *The RNLI flag...at half-mast...* "It brings home how dangerous the sea is and how vulnerable a community can be." 18th December 1999;
Father Noel Wynn, sm, Director, The National Shrine of Our Lady, Walsingham for *The Crib in the Chapel of Reconciliation, December 2001*;
Anne Reeve for *Christmas Eve at Mangreen*;
The Friends of Norwich Cathedral for *Norwich Cathedral Crib* by Josephina de Vasconcellos, photographed by Patrick Smith;
Langham Glass for their Norfolk Black turkey;

The Eastern Daily Press for *Caley's ladies making Christmas crackers in Norwich,5th December 1956*;

Allan Jones for *King's Lynn Ramblers walking on the Sandringham Estate, 2002*;

Tony Hall and *The Eastern Daily Press* for *"Which reminds me, dear - how'd you get on in the city today?"* 27th December 2001;

Rev. Canon Phillip McFadyen & Theresa Bloomfield for *The Church of St. Helen at Ranworth* photographed by Theresa Bloomfield;

The Eastern Daily Press for *Cinderella at Kings Lynn, 1968*;

Andrew Dodds for *The Church of St. Michael, Beccles*;

Tony Hall and *The Eastern Daily Press* for *"Bye-bye Christmas tree...."* 4th January 2001;

The National Trust for *Felbrigg Hall*;

and my thanks to the staff of the *EDP*'s library and picture archives.

Moya Leighton
2003

Useful Addresses

The Adrian Bell Society, John Ford, Chairman, Apple Acre, Church Lane, Claxton, Norfolk. NR14 7HY

Norah Brindid, Orfanon, The Green, Hickling, Norfolk. NR12 0XR

Jardine Press, The Round House, Lower Raydon, Hadleigh, Suffolk. IP7 5QN

Norfolk & Suffolk Research Group, 4 Paines Orchard, Cheddington, Bedfordshire. LU7 0SN

John Nursey, Forge Cottage, Flaxton, York. YO60 7RW

Stormforce Publications, Wild Water Holt, St. Ives, Cornwall. TR26 2HN

The Sylvia Townsend Warner Society, Eileen Johnson, Secretary, 2 Vicarage Lane, Fordington, Dorchester, Dorset. DT1 1LH

The Wildfowl & Wetlands Trust, Slimbridge, Gloucestershire. GL2 7BT

Henry Williamson Literary Estate, Keepers, West Dean Woods, Chichester, West Sussex. PO18 0RU